Grape Growing For Amateurs
Plain Instructions For the Successful Cultivation of Grapes

by Edwin Molyneux

with an introduction by Roger Chambers

This work contains material that was originally published in 1891.

This publication is within the Public Domain.

*This edition is reprinted for educational purposes
and in accordance with all applicable Federal Laws.*

Introduction Copyright 2018 by Roger Chambers

COVER CREDITS

Front Cover
Wine Grapes Baja by Tomás Castelazo (Own work)
[CC BY-SA 2.5 - https://creativecommons.org/licenses/by-sa/2.5],
via Wikimedia Commons

Back Cover
Ripe Grapes by Scott Bauer, *Agricultural Research Service / USDA*.
Image Number K7248-56
[Public domain],
via Wikimedia Commons

Research / Resources
Wikimedia Commons
www.Commons.Wikimedia.org

Many thanks to all the incredible photographers, artists,
researchers, biographers, historians, and archivists who share
their great work via the Wikipedia family.

PLEASE NOTE :
As with all reprinted books of this age that are intended to perfectly reproduce the original edition, considerable pains and effort had to be undertaken to correct fading and sometimes outright damage to existing proofs of this title. At times, this task can be quite monumental, requiring an almost total rebuilding of some pages from digital proofs of multiple copies. Despite this, imperfections still sometimes exist in the final proof and may detract slightly from the visual appearance of the text.

DISCLAIMER :
Due to the age of this book, some methods or practices may have been deemed unsafe or unacceptable in the interim years. In utilizing the information herein, you do so at your own risk. We republish antiquarian books without judgment or revisionism, solely for their historical and cultural importance, and for educational purposes.

Self Reliance Books

Get more historic titles on animal and stock breeding, gardening and old fashioned skills by visiting us at:

http://selfreliancebooks.blogspot.com/

introduction

Here at **Self-Reliance Books** we are dedicated to bringing you the best in *dusty-old-book-knowledge* to help you in your quest for self-sufficiency and food independence.

We're so pleased to bring you another title on Horticulture – this time a book on growing grapes for first-timers.

This special edition of **Grape Growing For Amateurs** was written by Edwin Molyneux in 1891, making it well over a century old.

The book features sections on *Forms of Vineries, Propagation, List of Varieties, First Year's Growth of Young Vines, Insect Pests and Diseases, Peculiarities of Some Varieties*, and more.

Some of the varieties covered includes *Black Hamburgh, Lady Downes, Alicante, Mrs. Pince, White Tokay, Trebbiano*, among others.

This fantastic old text is a great book to start with for all those embarking on growing their first Grape crop, and all those considering taking the plunge and entering the industry.

~ *Roger Chambers*
State of Jefferson, April 2018

PREFACE.

IN writing this little treatise for the benefit of the fast-increasing body of amateur cultivators, I have endeavoured to employ as plain language as possible, well knowing that many an enthusiast lacks the knowledge of detail upon which so much depends.

Given the means necessary, a rigid restriction to approved varieties—which I have carefully enumerated, more with an aim to reaping good results than to the forming of a collection of sorts—and a faithful carrying out *at all times* of the instructions which are given, and I venture to think that the amateur may assure himself of success in the cultivation of this the king of fruits.

E. M.

SWANMORE PARK GARDENS,
    BISHOP'S WALTHAM.

July, 1891.

CONTENTS.

CHAPTER		PAGE
I.	Introduction	1
II.	Forms of Vineries	4
III.	Borders and Soil	11
IV.	Propagation	16
V.	List of Varieties	22
VI.	Planting	32
VII.	Early Vinery Treatment	36
VIII.	Muscat Vinery Treatment	40
IX.	Late Vinery Treatment	43
X.	Greenhouse Treatment	47
XI.	Summer Treatment, Watering, Ventilation, &c.	49
XII.	First Year's Growth of Young Vines	56
XIII.	Manipulation of the Shoots	63
XIV.	Thinning the Bunches	67
XV.	Insect Pests and Diseases	77
XVI.	Shanking	84
XVII.	Bottling Grapes	88
XVIII.	Pruning	93
XIX.	Winter Treatment	99
XX.	Inarching Vines	104
XXI.	Renovating Old Borders	107
XXII.	Peculiarities of some Varieties	111
XXIII.	Liquid Stimulants during Winter	117
XXIV.	Multiplication of Branches	119
XXV.	Air Roots	121
	Index	123

GRAPE GROWING FOR AMATEURS.

CHAPTER I.

INTRODUCTION.

FROM what I know of amateurs and their wishes, I believe that there is no phase of horticultural pursuits that is more interesting, or in which there is a greater wish to excel, than Grape-growing; but at the same time there is no subject that is in a general way less understood in all its details than the art of producing good grapes. I do not mean to say that there are no exceptions, for there are to every rule, and I know amateurs who have just cause to be proud of their fruit, which would make many a professional gardener blush. What I mean is, that there is a great lack of knowledge of the details which it is necessary to know before the enthusiastic amateur cultivator can hope to take a high position on the exhibition table, if inclination leads him in that direction.

One great disadvantage that amateurs have to contend with, I know, is absence from home at some parts of the day when their presence is really necessary, especially during the spring, when air-giving causes so much trouble and time to be spent; and many crops of otherwise good fruit are lost, I fear, through inability to attend to the air-giving, say during the month of April, when the sun shines forth with great power for a short time, almost as quickly sulking behind a flitting cloud. It is by such variations as this causes that amateurs, whose vocations call them from home during the day, are so heavily handicapped compared with their brethren the professional gardeners; for I contend that it is just as easy to grow a dozen houses of grapes as it is one, providing, of course, the necessary means are available to meet the multiplication of the same duties and details.

Where amateurs as a rule err in management is in attempting to do too much in one vinery, which has often to do duty for not only a vinery, but for a greenhouse, stove, and fernery, as well. It is all very well to grow one or two of these subjects along with the vines, but it must not be those that are quite opposite in the matter of heat requirements. Where the amateur can provide himself with a vinery independent of either stove or greenhouse plants, he can certainly command success, and at the same time accommodate many other kinds of plants without any detriment, providing he make all else subservient to the grapes. Therefore, there is every reason why amateurs should follow the hobby successfully; and with the assistance of a few details of culture, which I will endeavour to give as clearly as possible, I trust many more may be induced to make a start in the production of their own grapes.

With glass-houses vines can be grown successfully anywhere, as they are not like subjects which need the open air half the year and thus feel the effects of adverse climatical influences; but under cover always, the amateur is practically independent even of those baneful influences which are so detrimental to the gardens of amateurs living near large towns.

I have but a poor opinion of out-door grape culture, for the seasons nowadays are so variable and so little adapted to insure success that I think the attempt to cultivate a crop of even decent grapes is but labour uselessly expended, especially when it is considered what a number of other fruits there are which would succeed in the same position, and with but very little trouble expended on them, compared with that required for vines in the open.

From the foregoing remarks, it will be gathered that I advise amateurs not to attempt out-door grape culture, but to lay the foundation for house culture in a proper manner—that is, having properly-constructed houses, well-made borders, and suitable varieties—and by giving close attention to necessary details of culture, success may even be secured where the structural accommodation is not of the best.

CHAPTER II

FORMS OF VINERIES.

CIRCUMSTANCES so much affect the arrangement and construction of vineries—whether they shall be of one form or another, and upon what scale they shall be erected—that all I can do here is to point out the most suitable forms and their advantages, leaving their construction to individual tastes and requirements.

The commonest form of vinery is the lean-to, as represented by Fig. 1, for the reason that it is generally the most easily built and costs less than any other form, because in nine cases out of ten the back wall is already built, and brickwork is generally quite as expensive as wood and glass. Another advantage which the lean-to has over other forms, when it is situated with a southern aspect, is that less fire-heat is needed than for any other, because it is not so liable to be affected by wind; while span-roofed houses are much subjected to strong winds (especially in the spring, when the wind often blows from an easterly direction), owing to the manner in which they are exposed, as it is necessary for this form of house to be in such a position as to receive sufficient light on both sides of it. The lean-to house is the best where a combination of vinery and greenhouse has to be effected, as the back part of the house admits of a good-sized stage for plants. The size of such a house depends entirely upon the requirements and means of the owner. The following dimensions make a good-sized house, large enough to accommodate seven early vines or six late ones. This is a very good guide as to what is needed by individuals. Length, 24ft.; width, 12ft.; height at back, 13ft.; height at the front, 5ft.; all measurements being taken from the ground level.

Where a vinery is to be built especially for grapes as the first consideration, and with a view to producing them in the best possible form, I most strongly recommend Fig. 2,

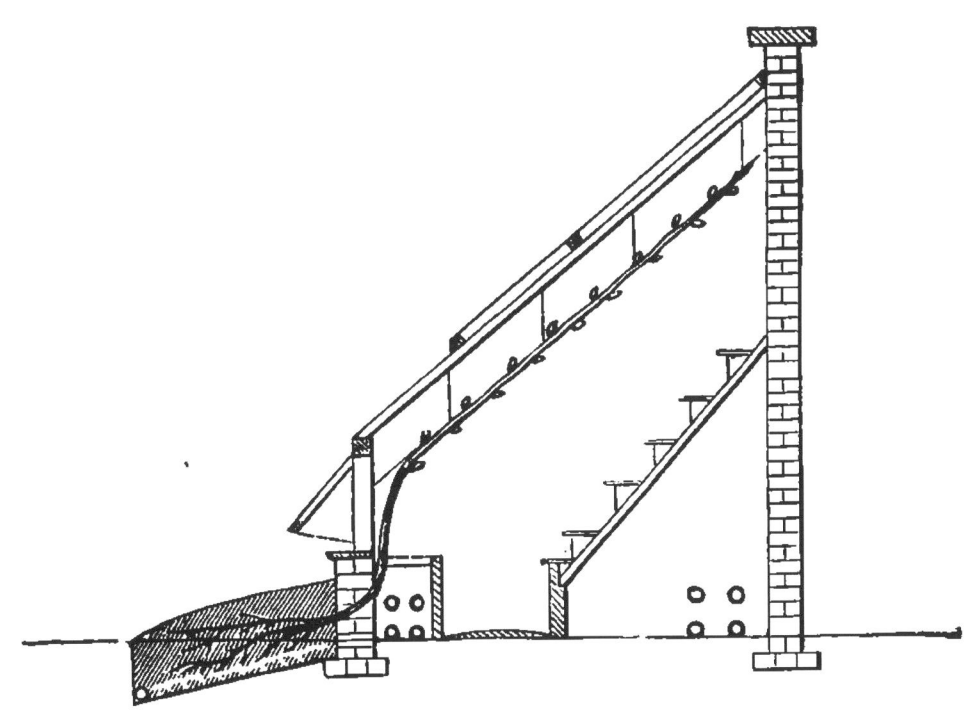

FIG. 1. LEAN-TO VINERY.

which is best known under the name of a "three-quarter span." The back light is such a useful addition to the ordinary lean-to that it is certainly worth adopting. One advantage gained is, additional light through the roof for the vines, and for any plants or climbers it is desired to grow at the base of the back wall, as these when trained up the wall have a much better chance of succeeding than when under the vines, as they are in the lean-to. Another advantage is that if the lights are made to be movable air can be admitted to the house without injury even should the wind be blowing too strong from the south-east, as it very often is in the spring when the vines are in bloom, and when this wind would be most injurious to the bunches just setting. It is not a good plan to admit air to a vinery from two opposite directions, which causes a draught, and this is to be avoided in grape culture. Underneath the back light, shelves

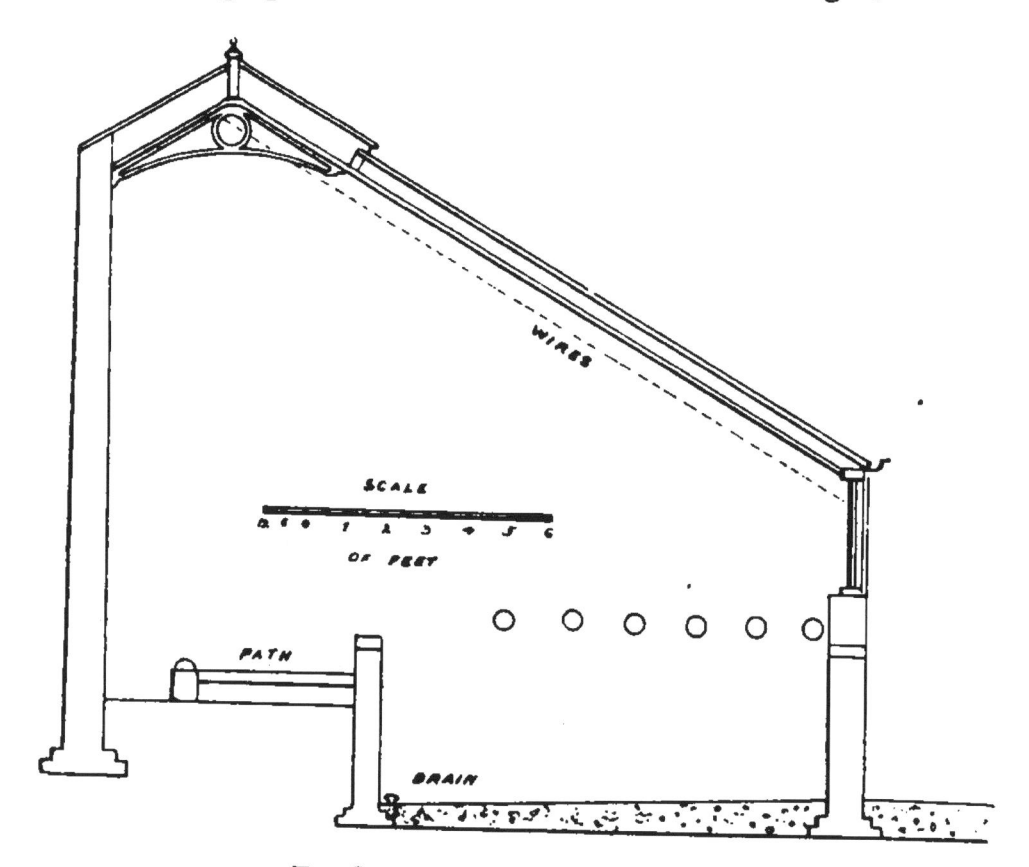

FIG. 2. THREE-QUARTER-SPAN VINERY.

can also be suspended from the rafters, and they are useful for many things: French beans, or strawberries, for instance, succeed well. The dimensions of a very good size three-quarter-span house are: length, 27ft.; width, 18ft.; height from floor line to ridge, 14ft.; height of front lights, 2ft.; length of the back lights, 4ft.; and height of the back wall, 12ft. 6in. A house this size will accommodate eight early vines or seven late ones.

Fig. 3 represents a span-roof vinery, which is perhaps the most economically constructed of all, when the additional roof space is taken into consideration; but the site required for a house of this form is not always available. One advantage of span-roof houses is that some part of them obtains the sun's rays all day, except, of course, when the site is unfavourable, which it should not be, as a suitable site is an important factor in successful grape culture. That facing the south is the best of all; a south-westerly position is fairly good, and so is one facing the east, providing the cultivator is an early riser: in the contrary event, the vines

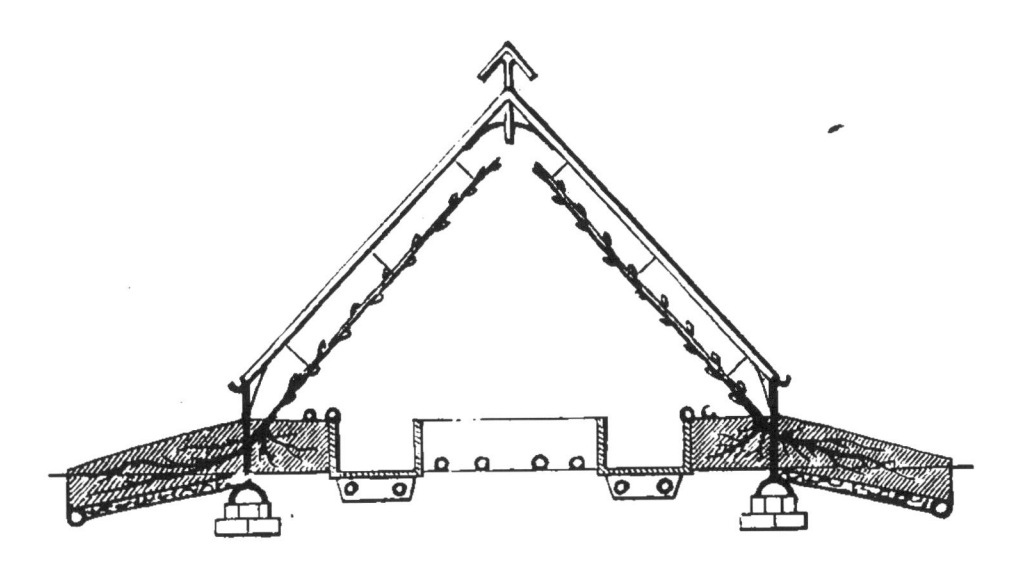

FIG. 3. SPAN-ROOF VINERY.

run a great risk of being scorched, as during the summer such a house would be found very hot early in the morning. Some of the best grapes I have ever seen were the produce of a vinery facing east, but it was under the charge of a most noted grape-grower, Mr. J. Meredith, of Garston Vineyard, near Liverpool. Span-roof vineries should run north and south, so as to have the sun upon them all day in some place or other. In whatever form the house may be built, it is essential for the roof to be pitched sharp so that the sun may have more power on it than when the slope is flatter. The difference between the two styles will be discernible inside the house in the colour of the fruit, for grapes do not colour so well under a roof which is nearly flat as they do when the roof is pitched sharper, the reason being quite obvious. The glass should be quite clear and of 21oz. weight, for the roof.

The manner in which the vinery is to be heated requires some consideration. In the case of the lean-to, as shown in Fig. 1, the pipes must of necessity be fixed underneath the front stage, so as not to interfere with the growth and arrangement of plants upon the stages, both back and front of the house. In the case of the three-quarter span (Fig. 2), which is meant to be treated as a vinery proper, the arrangement of the pipes differs from any other style of house. The hot-water pipes should be spread over the surface of the inside border, as shown on section of Fig. 2. Six rows of 4in. pipes would suffice to maintain the necessary heat at all times and all stages of growth, unless the position were much exposed to easterly winds. It is mistaken economy to provide a vinery with too few hot-water pipes, for more fuel is required to make the few pipes hot enough to sustain sufficient heat than is needed to warm them where there is a larger number; neither is it good for the vines when the pipes have to be made so hot that the hand cannot be placed on them without experiencing a sense of burning. The advantage of spreading the hot-water pipes over the whole of the surface of the border is that the heat from them is more equalised throughout the vinery than it would be if they were clustered together along the front of the house, as in this case the heat from the pipes ascending directly to the vines is often the means of covering the foliage with red-spider, owing to the continued dry atmosphere under the leaves in this particular spot. The hot-water pipes in all cases should be 4in. in diameter, and should be so fixed that a quick rise in the flow of the water is obtained—say 1in. in 24ft., which will suffice to cause a free circulation. Where the pipes are spread over the border as explained above, the arrangement should be five flow-pipes and one return-pipe, for this method insures the quickest circulation the water can have, and at the same time creates an equable temperature which will secure an even growth in all the vines alike. The vinery should be provided with valves on both flow- and return-pipes, as these are the surest means of commanding the temperature of the house at all times.

Provision should be made under the roof to secure the vines both when in active growth and when dormant during the season of rest. There is no plan so successful as wires properly fixed to the rafters. Some persons have the wires arranged in such a manner that when the leaves are fully grown, there is not sufficient space for them next the glass. The consequence is that they get scorched, which is detrimental to the vines, by checking that free growth so desirable at all times during activity; besides which, the appearance of a vinery with scorched leaves does not speak well for the management of it. Galvanised wire, No. 8 size, should be stretched horizontally across the house 1ft. 4in. from the glass for early varieties, and 2in. more for the late vinery, and kept in place by means of thin iron screw eyelets fixed to the underneath side of the rafters, the wires threaded through the holes, and made tight at one end with the aid of a nut and a screw fitted at one end of the house to a support made from angle iron; the opposite end of the wire should be secured to a fixed bar on the rafter forming the end of the house. A distance of 10in. should be allowed between each wire, which gives ample opportunity for securing both side-growths and bunches alike.

In the case of the combined greenhouse and vinery, where the vines are planted wider apart so as to admit sun and light between the vines for the benefit of the plants growing underneath them, the wires should be fixed so that they run parallel with the rafters, and should be three in number; the centre wire is to secure the main rod or stem, and the two sides ones are intended for the young growth, which is trained in a horizontal fashion. The three wires should be the same distance from the glass as given in the preceding paragraph, and 10in. from each other.

To prevent any damage to the tender vine shoots through coming in contact with the galvanised wire, it is a good plan to give the wire a couple of coats of white paint, which removes all fear in this direction. I have seen whole shoots die off through no other cause, and this makes a bad gap in the vine unless precautions are taken to prevent it.

CHAPTER III.

BORDERS AND SOIL.

THE making of a border for the growth of vines is one of the most important points to study in grape culture, for without a properly-constructed border it is impossible to grow good grapes for any length of time; therefore, the work should be done in a thorough manner at first, with a view to many years of success with the same vines. The great fault many persons fall into is the constructing of their borders too deeply, too much soil being employed, which is wrong for two reasons—the cost of conveyance is greater, and the opportunity given of allowing too much space for the roots to penetrate deeply, which deprives them of the warmth from sun-heat they would obtain if the border were shallower and the roots nearer to the surface.

A border, whether indoors or out, should be raised well above the level of the surrounding ground, to admit of easy drainage and of the roots obtaining the benefit of solar heat. The loss of sun-heat to the roots in early spring which is consequent on too great depth of the borders is a cause of shanking in many instances, and this is one of the greatest evils a grape-grower has to contend against. A depth of 2ft. of soil is ample for any vine border.

Fig. 4 gives a good idea of how the border is to be made. Where space will admit on the outside of the vinery, it is a good plan to have a border there as well as inside—a combination of inside and outside,—for the reason that a less width is required inside the house for the roots to ramble in, thus admitting of more space for plants or other things. A border 6ft. wide inside is ample if another one outside can be formed 8ft. wide; and these, if properly made at the start, will maintain the vines in good condition for at least twenty years.

In making a new border, it is not wise to complete it at once; rather make it piecemeal, by adding a couple of feet in width every year until the limit is reached. The vines will thus obtain more support, by their roots being able to

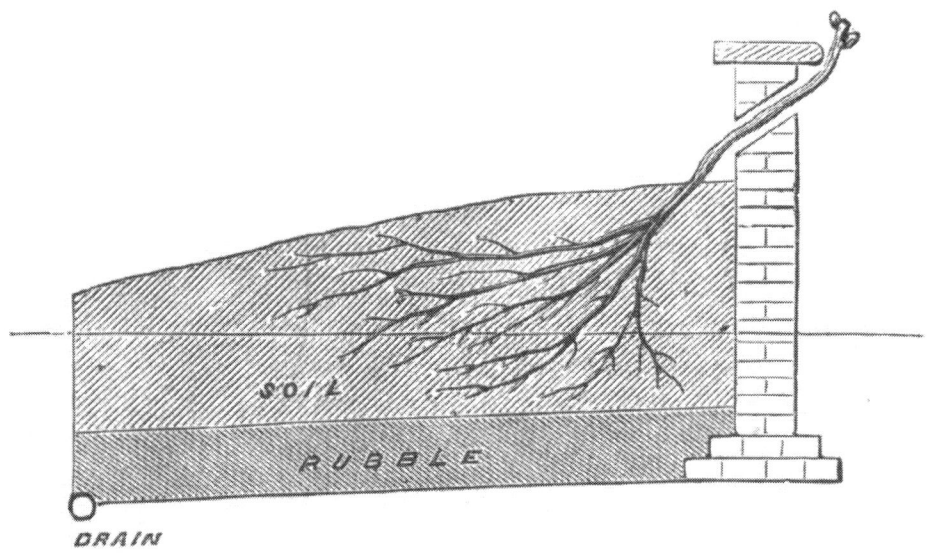

FIG. 4. VINE BORDER.

run into new soil. This plan is better for the soil also; for when the border is made up its whole width at first, the fibrous matter contained in the turf used decays before the vines have had the opportunity of receiving any benefit from its use; whereas by adding to its width annually, each part of it is utilised properly by the roots for the benefit of the vines.

If the border is to be a combination, arches should be built in the front wall when the vinery is made, and through these the roots will run into the outside border. Of course, it will be seen that the vines should be planted inside the house, which is best where they are the chief consideration. For the first year's growth, an inside border 3ft. wide and the same width outside will suffice for a start.

Where there is any risk of the roots penetrating into the subsoil below the border it is a good plan to concrete the base of it, which effectually brings them under control. The making of this base need not be a costly affair, as any handy labourer can do the work sufficiently well: a thickness of 4in. will suffice. It should be formed of broken stones or brick rubble with a small portion of sand and Portland cement or lime mixed with it, making the whole wet enough to adhere together when well rammed down with an iron rammer; and it should be made with a correct slope from the inside wall to the back of the border, as shown on Fig. 4. From this slope the water will be conveyed into a drain running along the foot of the border and connected with a similar drain in the outside border, which should be formed in the same manner as the inside one. Some persons lay cross drains at the base of the border lengthwise across it; but if it has a quick slope from the wall to the front, and plenty of drainage, such as stones or broken bricks, there is not the slightest necessity for more drains than the one along the front, both inside and outside. The borders must be enclosed with a low retaining wall, to prevent the roots rambling beyond control. When the border is fully made up to this wall it is a good plan to insert a few perpendicular drain-pipes close to it, to admit air down to the drainage, which will maintain both soil and wall in a sweet condition.

The depth of the borders should be so made that 1ft. of rubble or stones can be employed on the top of the concrete base with 2ft. depth of soil; and if 1ft. of the latter is above the surface of the surrounding level, so much the better, especially if the natural soil be of a heavy description, for this is always much colder during the winter, spring, and autumn than where the natural soil is inclined to be of a sandy nature.

Where it is impossible to have an outside as well as an inside border owing to circumstances, the inside one should not be less than 10ft. wide, if the vinery is of the same size as shown on Fig. 2; but a border 6ft. wide inside and an outside one 10ft. wide will be ample, and should be made in yearly additions of 2ft. width. This is done by building a wall of turf on the top of the drainage, which will retain the given soil inside; and in October, or whenever it is convenient to make the addition to the border, the wall of turf can be removed, if not so much permeated with roots that its removal would cause them injury, in which case it must remain and become part of the border uninterrupted.

It matters little whether the borders be made during the months of November, February, March, or April, so long as the soil with which this is done is in a proper state for use—neither too wet nor too dry; but as March or early in April is perhaps the best period in which to plant vines, I should prefer the borders to be made about one month before that time, so that the soil might have an opportunity of getting settled down firmly, that when the vines were planted they would not eventually be too deep in the border in consequence of the settling of the soil and frequent top-dressings afterwards with soil and manure.

The best compost to use is turf fresh cut from a pasture or deer park; failing this material the best soil that can be had must be used, mixing with it suitable additions in greater proportions than would be necessary were turf obtained. To every cart-load of turf freshly cut, 3in. thick, and chopped into pieces 4in. and 6in. square, add one-sixth part of lime-rubbish, wood-ashes, broken bricks, and charcoal, limiting the quantity of the first and last in proportion to the kind of loam to be used. For instance, if this be of a heavy, close, retentive nature, more of the ingredients named will be required to maintain the porosity of the soil; but where the loam is inclined to be of a sandy nature, less of them will be needed. To each load of the mixture, whether it be heavy or light, add ¼cwt. of ½in. ground bones. These ingredients may be added in making up the border, which is preferable to mixing the whole together previously, because by constant turnings over of the compost to as thoroughly incorporate as is thought to be necessary, the loam or soil becomes broken up so finely as to lose much of its porous nature when put together, and consequently is more liable to become inert and too close to admit of a rapid discharge of the water which of necessity must be applied copiously from time to time for the support of the immense quantity of foliage which healthy vines carry.

The border should be made in the following manner: From 10in. to 1ft. of broken bricks or stones should be laid as openly as possible on the concrete base, building up the outside of the bed as squarely as possible so that no difficulty may be experienced in making the retaining wall of turfs, to prevent the finer soil from washing outwards as might be the case were the borders made piecemeal. Over the drainage of stones or bricks, lay one layer of turfs with the grassy side downwards: this will prevent the fine soil from running down amongst the drainage, which would in time block the water passage and cause a stagnation in the border that would ultimately end in the grapes shanking.

The necessity of preparing the foundation of the border carefully will be apparent now that I have pointed out the evils which will ensue if the work be done in a careless manner; and any extra time spent in this will be found advantageous in after years.

If the compost be put in the border in layers, as suggested, in preference to mixing all the ingredients together, a layer of lime-rubbish or charcoal should commence on the top of the upturned turfs covering the drainage; proceed in layers of first one sort, then another, until the border is made the requisite height, which should be quite 6in. above that which it is ultimately intended to be; at the same time tread the soil down quite firm, if it be in the right condition of moisture—that is, neither wet nor dry.

CHAPTER IV.

PROPAGATION.

THERE are several methods of propagating vines, but except in peculiar circumstances it is not at all necessary to resort to more than one way, viz., from eyes. This plan of increasing the stock of any variety is much the best, both in point of convenience and utility, and for the rapidity with which plants can be raised suitable for planting in new vineries or for growing in pots. Any one with limited convenience need experience but the slightest difficulty in raising a stock of vines. All that is required is the means of providing a gentle bottom heat, and afterwards a warm house for a time, while during the summer an ordinary greenhouse will suffice to complete the growth. Cuttings are sometimes employed, but on account of the uncertainty of their rooting freely, and the manner in which they go off afterwards below the ground line, it is useless troubling with them; besides which, more than one growth from the base of a vine is neither necessary nor desirable for any form of culture; and as that is to be obtained from a single eye there is no necessity for employing cuttings to produce new plants. The only other form of what must be termed propagation is that named "inarching," which is the substitution of one variety for another in an already established vinery.

Supposing that any particular kind, after a thorough trial of say five years, does not give satisfaction, or does not please the palate of the owner, instead of rooting out the whole plant and replacing it with another variety, it is much better to inarch the new kind upon the stock of the established cane, as greater success would be achieved in the changing of the kinds than would be the case were a young vine planted, as small canes never make satisfactory progress in an old border. I purpose dealing with the question of inarching in a separate chapter, as, although it may not take up much space, it is of sufficient importance to merit a separate heading.

In my opinion, then, the only method of propagating the vine, besides inarching, is by eyes, and for the reasons stated above. The great point in selecting the eyes is to take them from a reliable source as to distinctness of name, and where the vines have previously produced satisfactory results. If the after-treatment then is correct, success with the future crop cannot but be assured. The shoots selected should be of the current year's growth, not too strong, as these would contain too much pith in the stems; neither should they be too weak: medium-sized hard growths are the best, and are sure to be well ripened. The branches as here described may be cut from the plant any time after the leaves have fallen, and should be at once laid in some soil out of doors, just covering with soil the base where cut from the vine, to maintain them fresh until the time arrives for inserting the eyes, which is best done as soon after New Year's Day as possible.

Fig. 5 represents an eye of Black Hamburgh prepared for insertion in the pots. Take a shoot, select a suitable eye (which should be plump and have the appearance of making a perfect

FIG. 5. EYE PREPARED FOR INSERTION.

growth, avoiding eyes which have been in any way damaged so that the skin which covers the bud is broken, as this is almost certain to produce disappointing results), hold the eye firmly in the left hand, and with a sharp knife cut the under-side of the shoot in a slanting direction, terminating about 1in. from the bud, as shown in the engraving; reverse the shoot, and cut in a similar manner in the opposite direction. Pare the edges of the bark smoothly, which will facilitate root formation. Prepare a sufficient number of 2½in. pots, first by washing them thoroughly clean; then at the bottom over the hole in the pot place a single crock, large enough to cover the hole; on this lay a few pieces of partly-decayed leaves, to prevent the small soil washing down and blocking up the passage way for water about the crock. The pots should be three-parts filled with a compost of two parts of fibry loam, one part of leaf soil, and a sixth part of silver sand, passing all through a fine-mesh sieve. Press it down firmly, and insert the eye as shown by Fig. 6, with just the bud showing above the soil. If the soil be moist, as it should be, no water will be required beyond a sprinkle to settle the soil on the surface about the eye. Stand the pots on a moist base, plunging them in ashes, sand, or cocoanut fibre refuse, which will maintain the soil in the pots in a moist state. On the stage of the greenhouse or vinery, where the necessary plunging material can be secured, will suffice for two or three weeks, after which period a slight bottom heat must be given to induce the eyes to break into growth and make roots freely: a hotbed, propagating case, or any place where a bottom heat of 60deg. can be had to start with, increasing it to 70deg. in two or three weeks time. I have met with good results in rooting the eyes on the top of the hot-water pipes in an early vinery; and this answers well where the pipes are clustered together along the front of the house, and at a reasonable distance from the glass, so that the new growth does not become drawn up weakly at the start—a thing to be avoided. By laying some slates on the hot-water pipes, to prevent the plunging material falling through between the pipes, and by fixing a lath about 3in. or 4in. wide

FIG. 6. EYE INSERTED IN POT.

around the edges for the same purpose, success will be certain. If the vinery is started by the middle of January, the heat required for that purpose will be just the thing for giving bottom heat to the vine eyes in the production of roots; and, as the vinery progresses, so will the eyes receive the benefit of more heat, consequent on the hot-water pipes being made hotter to maintain the temperature of the vinery at different stages of growth. To avoid excess of heat at the base of the pots, a greater depth of plunging material may be employed.

The position just described is one which shows how the difficulty of obtaining bottom heat may be overcome by the amateur cultivator. Where this can be secured without the necessity of adopting such means as here stated, an advantage is obtained; but the amateur often has to labour under difficulties little known to cultivators in other branches of gardening. Even by plunging the pots in material such as described in the evaporating troughs in the vinery success can be secured.

The soil in the pots must never be allowed to become dry, but be maintained in a moist state. Tepid water should always be given, as cold would have a tendency to chill the soil and roots growing in a warm position, and would give a check to that free growth so desirable right from the time when the bud makes its first signs of life until the season's growth is complete.

When the pots are nearly full of roots, and in most cases when that has been accomplished the plants will have a single stem to each, varying in length from 1in. to 3in., they are ready for their first shift into 4in. pots, using the same kind of soil as recommended for the eyes, except that it must not be made quite so fine; passing it through a ½in. sieve will this time suffice. The soil should be well warmed preparatory to using, to avoid a check to growth, as the tender roots are very susceptible to checks of this kind by anything cold coming in contact with them. Return the pots to the bottom-heat position for a time until new growth is made at the roots; afterwards, a position near the glass will answer best, and if a moist base can be provided so much the better. Upon no account should the roots be allowed to suffer for want of water, or red spider and thrip will soon attack the foliage; and these are not only most difficult to eradicate, but cause a check to the growth.

When the roots reach the sides of the pots, and before they are in any way pot-bound, larger pots must be provided for them: those 10in. in diameter are best for the stronger, and those an inch less for the weaker plants. The compost for this potting should consist of three parts of fibry loam, one part of partly decayed horse-droppings, and a good sprinkling of old lime rubbish, especially if the loam is inclined to be heavy in character. A depth of 2in. of drainage should be allowed for each pot, and broken pots or bricks is the best material for this purpose. Over the drainage lay some of the rougher parts of the compost, to prevent the fine soil washing down and blocking the passage way for future waterings. In turning the plants out of the pots, be careful that the roots are not damaged, and press the soil firmly about them, allowing a space of 1½in. at the top for subsequent waterings, as abundance will be required when these pots are filled with roots. Place beside each plant a thin stake, to which the growth should be tied as fast as made, preserving it in an upright direction.

The plants should have a position where plenty of light and sun can be afforded, so that the growth will be short-jointed, stocky, and firm as it proceeds. The temperature should not fall below 60deg. at any time until growth is complete in the autumn; and draughts of cold air should at all times be avoided, as they predispose to mildew, which is about the worst enemy a vine can have.

The foliage should be syringed twice daily with tepid water, early in the morning and again in the afternoon, closing the house early to insure a moist, growing atmosphere, which vines revel in, although they appreciate abundant supplies of fresh air when admitted in a regular manner.

When the pots are full of roots, copious supplies of weak

liquid manure should be applied alternately with clear water. By no means should the plants suffer for want of water at the roots, nor should the atmosphere of the house be kept dry during the growing period. All lateral growths should be promptly pinched off, retaining the upright growth of the stem intact. When the canes by the colour of their bark show signs of ripening and the leaves show signs of maturity, abundance of air should be admitted to the house day and night for two or three weeks, and afterwards the plants should be removed out of doors, standing the pots on a thick bed of ashes or boards at the foot of a south wall, where they will obtain ample sunlight and warmth to enable them to attain a perfect ripening of the wood. The canes should be secured to the wall, and the roots kept moist, but not wet, which would defeat the object in view, viz., the thorough maturing of the canes. Here the vines may remain until they are required for planting early in the year, if the pots are entirely covered with straw or litter, or anything else which will prevent the roots becoming frozen. No water after this time will be required at the roots, as they will obtain from other sources sufficient moisture to maintain the soil in a moist state; but the roots should never be allowed to become dry, or they will shrivel, and many will die in consequence.

CHAPTER V.

LIST OF VARIETIES.

IN choosing the varieties of grapes to be planted, I shall bear in mind their utility for various purposes, and not enumerate a list of fanciful kinds which have little to recommend them beyond novelty of some form or other. For the amateur cultivator such kinds as those last named are a nuisance rather than benefit, because those that are worthless from a cultivator's point of view require just as much time and attention bestowed upon them as do those sorts which can be depended upon to produce a crop of seasonable grapes which can be enjoyed, after all the labour and anxiety expended upon their growth. The amateur is so seldom in a position to enable him to dabble with novelties of any kind about which there is a doubt of their future value as crop producers that he of all persons should steer clear of such fancies, and much better is it for him to cultivate one or two well-known good kinds from which, with reasonable attention, he may reckon upon a crop of fruit. Open-air grapes now-a-days can be so little depended upon to ripen that it is useless to take up space with more than one or two kinds, which I will mention for the benefit of cultivators who still adhere to the open-air method of culture.

I propose to place the kinds in sections suitable for the various houses, giving the better ones at the head of each list, so that any person may choose from those named as many kinds as required, always commencing at the top.

I will just give a descriptive list of varieties and their uses, with points of excellence noted, afterwards making a selection for the various purposes, as by this manner of dealing with them much repetition will be avoided. Dividing them into two sections—Black and White kinds—I will commence with the Black varieties.

BLACK.

Black Hamburgh.—This is the most generally cultivated variety in existence, yet none that I know is more seldom

FIG. 7. BLACK HAMBURGH GRAPES.

seen in first-rate condition. It is one of the easiest grapes to grow in a moderate manner, succeeding in either a hot or cold house; but at exhibitions it generally lacks the highest points of excellence—size of berry and high colour—for which it is noted when at its best. As a cool-house grape there is none to equal it. In flavour, when in good condition, it is excellent, and at all points, without doubt, the finest variety individually in cultivation, as it will either force very early, or can be grown without any artificial heat whatever. It is, however, liable to be troubled with two of the greatest ills that can befall grape-growers—shanking and red spider. This, of course, happening under moderate treatment; but that which is suitable to this variety prevents either of these drawbacks from making any headway.

I have thought it well to point out those ills which this variety is heir to, as well as its good points; therefore, by avoiding those which are bad, the good qualities may be obtained. The bunches are medium in size, and one weighing 4lb. is considered large for the kind; the berries are roundish-ovate; the skin, bluish-black, covered with a deep bloom; flesh, firm, tender, and juicy, with a nice flavour. It is a free-setting kind.

Madresfield Court.—As an individual bunch this is the finest black grape in existence; but as a general crop, under any conditions, it is not so serviceable as the preceding variety. The bunches are long, tapering, in most cases evenly shouldered, although some bunches will have a very large shoulder on one side, the berries are very large, purplish-black, and carry a good bloom; the skin is thin; the flavour a strong Muscat taste. It is a vigorous-growing kind, yet does not produce wood of large size. Its worst fault is that, where cultural conditions are not suitable, the berries split across the point just at the time when they are colouring. It will succeed in a perfectly cool house, is a good forcing variety, or is equally good when ripened with the latest of kinds; therefore it can be had in good condition from June to November, which is over a long stretch of time.

Lady Downes is perhaps the finest late grape in cultivation, not on account of the size of its bunches and berries, but for the excellent colour the latter assume and the length of time which they will keep fresh and maintain their flavour. I have seen well-preserved bunches of this variety in the August following its being ripe in October the year previous. No other grape will do this. At all times the flavour is good; but for its late-keeping qualities it is much valued. The bunches are rather below medium size, generally carrying a good shoulder, which for appearance sake is best removed early. The berries are quite round, very even in size, black, and carry a dense bloom. It is a free bearer, and with heat sets freely. The vine is a robust grower. It has a strong tendency to have the skin of its berries scalded about the time when they are stoning, which can be prevented by a systematic course of air-giving early in the morning, to dissipate the atmospheric moisture which condenses on the skin of the berry. The action of the sun upon this causes scalding to take place, which not only disfigures the bunch, but also materially reduces its weight, as berries so affected are quite useless afterwards.

Alicante.—This is another late variety, easy of cultivation —much more so than Lady Downes. The bunches are very large, and thickly set with berries, which are a true ovate shape and carry a very dense bloom; the colour is quite black. The bunches are often ill-shapen, having somewhat ugly-looking shoulders. The stems are short. The skin of the berries is very thick, but the flavour is fairly good in well-ripened samples. This variety is easily known from all others by the woolly appearance of the bark and leaf-stems, and by its compact yet vigorous growth. It is perhaps the most showy of all grapes.

Gros Colman produces the largest berries of any sort. It is a great bearer, and when seen in proper condition is of noble appearance. This grape is now largely used for market growing, commanding perhaps the highest price of any sort early in the spring. The flavour is only moderately good, but for invalids it is regarded as a capital sort, the skin being thin and the berries possessing so much flesh—not in any way tough. Generally, the bunches have a good-sized shoulder to each. The berries set freely, are quite round, deep black, and have a dense bloom when seen at its best. It requires heat to finish the ripening satisfactorily.

Gros Guillaume.—This is sometimes known as BARBAROSSA; in fact, it is more often called the latter name than the former. Those who are fond of sensational bunches of grapes will do well to cultivate this variety. Bunches are produced up to 20lb. weight; but one weighing even 10lb. is a fine sight. Of that size the berries colour well and carry a fine thick bloom. The bunches, large and small, are very shapely, being evenly shouldered and tapering. The vine is a strong grower, requiring rather more space than any other variety. Towards the end of August the foliage assumes beautiful autumnal tints of colour, and is very useful for the decoration of dessert dishes for, say, apples and pears. The berries of this grape are quite round, and of medium size, but moderate in flavour. They keep well, and keeping improves their taste a good deal.

Muscat Hamburgh.—When well grown this is a splendid grape—perhaps the finest-flavoured of any in cultivation; but it is such an uncertain kind to succeed that it is decidedly risky to plant even one vine of it in a limited space. In the first place, it is such a bad setter that many of the berries are stoneless, consequent upon the imperfect fertilisation of the flowers which require artificial aid in dispersing the pollen. Then, again, the berries show a tendency to shank, which quite spoils their appearance. The berries are long ovate, of good size, jet black with a dense bloom; flesh, firm and rich, with a decided Muscat flavour. The bunches are large, heavily shouldered, and freely produced.

Mrs. Pince.—This belongs to the Muscat-flavoured section of grapes. It hangs well, and is therefore valuable. The bunches are very shapely, being well proportioned, long, and tapering. The berries are medium-sized, ovate, purplish-black, and when perfect are densely coated with bloom; but so seldom is this sort seen in perfection, that when it is, it is much more valuable. As a rule it has a "foxey" appearance, failing to colour beyond the red stage. It also needs artificial aid in setting the bloom to have even-shaped bunches, and it certainly requires plenty of heat to effect its successful culture. It is of moderately strong growth, only requiring an ordinary amount of space.

Trentham Black is a capital variety for the amateur with limited means to grow. The bunches are very freely produced, the berries setting plentifully with just a little trouble. The former are medium-sized, long, and tapering; the latter medium also, ovate, and purplish-black. The flavour is especially vinous; and it is particularly liked by some in preference to any other for the strongly pronounced flavour in that direction. It hangs well. This is a variety which can, with impunity, be heavier cropped perhaps than any other.

Gros Maroc.—This is a very showy grape. No variety that I know puts on such a dense bloom as does this sort. The bunches are rather small; the berries large, nearly round, flattened at the end, and very closely packed on the bunch. The flavour is inclined to be acid, and only moderate. As a show variety for colour it stands high, but for table use it is inferior to so many other kinds that it is not worth growing. It is of medium growth.

Alnwick Seedling is another grape of excellent appearance when seen in good condition; but, unfortunately, this is seldom the case, owing to its disposition to produce so many small berries, the result of imperfect fertilisation. I have seen many bunches of this sort with not a single perfect berry in them. In good hands, too, in some seasons, it does not set properly. The bunches are generally furnished with one large shoulder; the berries are medium-sized, round, rather flat at the end, black, and carry a dense bloom; the skin is thick; the flavour fairly good when well ripened and kept awhile. It is a good keeper, but should only be grown for variety.

Black Morocco is a richly-flavoured kind, but generally not well coloured—purplish-red more often than black. The berries are generally thinly set.

Mill Hill Hamburgh is sometimes taken for the BLACK HAMBURGH, but is much inferior to that variety, both in point of flavour (which is decidedly inferior), setting qualities, and colour. Seldom do we see this kind well finished. It is not a desirable kind to grow, for the reasons given.

WHITE.

Good varieties of White grapes are not so plentiful as Black ones, neither need they be, for they are not nearly so much in favour as those of the other colour. There are but few kinds which grow with the aid of little fire heat, and most of them prefer warmth.

Muscat of Alexandria heads the list, both in point of quality and appearance, as when seen in its proper condition no variety can equal it. But seldom do we see this sort grown as well as it is possible to be. No sort that I am acquainted with shows the effect of mismanagement so soon as this does. It is absolutely a warm-house grape. The bunches are large, as also are the berries, which are long ovate, and golden amber when fully ripe. The flesh is firm, juicy, and sweet, with a high Muscat flavour.

Foster's Seedling is certainly the amateur's White grape. It is of easy culture, vigorous in growth, and produces bunches in abundance. The berries are not large, but set very freely. This variety requires a lot of thinning, and ripens its fruit equally well in a warm or cool house. The bunches are medium-sized and evenly shouldered. The berries are oval in shape, sweet, and melting.

Buckland Sweetwater produces large bunches and berries, but not so freely as does FOSTER'S SEEDLING, and some vines are sparsely cropped. When the vines are young, the bunches are straggly, gaining compactness with age and as they become more established in the border. The berries are nearly round, and generally pale green; but when thoroughly well ripened are amber coloured. With age, when over-ripe, they assume a dull white, which is a sign that it is time they were cut, as they soon lose flavour as well as appearance. Buckland Sweetwater is not considered remarkable for high quality; but the skin of the berries is crisp, while the flesh is juicy, sweet, and watery.

White Frontignan is a splendid variety to cultivate where a heavy crop with little trouble is preferred. Abundance of bunches, which are cylindrical in form, are produced, and set their berries very freely. These are quite round, the colour being pale yellow or greenish-white; the flesh is crisp, juicy, and well flavoured. This variety is deserving of extended cultivation, on account of its flavour; but owing to the small size of its berries, it has but a limited cultivation.

Duchess of Buccleuch is considered by some to be the highest-flavoured grape in cultivation; and it certainly has won many prizes for flavour only. In style of growth it resembles the preceding kind, except that the berries are larger. The colour of these is greenish-white.

Duke of Buccleuch has caused perhaps more correspondence than any other variety regarding its quality; and it is, probably, also a kind that is more difficult to cultivate than any other. It is the producer of the largest berries of any sort I am acquainted with. The bunches are rather small, and the berries nearly round; the colour is greenish-yellow; flavour, sweet, with tender flesh, and very juicy. Where it succeeds it is an excellent early variety, growing well with BLACK HAMBURGH.

Cannon Hall Muscat is a noble-looking grape when in good condition, but seldom is this the case. It is such a shy setter that oftener than otherwise less than half the number of berries are found upon a bunch. The berries are exceedingly large for a Muscat and of capital flavour, but they are difficult to manage well.

Golden Queen is a fairly good late grape. The bunches are shapely, tapering, and evenly shouldered; the berries of fair size, and of a peculiar dull colour, not at all taking in appearance.

Trebbiano has very large, shapely bunches, which set freely and shank very badly, this spoiling its effect. The fruit has a brisk rather than high flavour; keeps well, and does not shrivel. It is noted as having produced the largest bunch of grapes of any kind; one, weighing 26¼lb., being shown in Scotland by Mr. Curror, of Eskbank.

White Tokay.—This is a free-producing as well as a free-setting variety, but very seldom do we see it other than a whitish-green. It requires to be well ripened before it is even moderately good in flavour. The vine is a strong grower, not much cultivated now.

More varieties might be mentioned, but as it would be merely for the sake of variety I refrain from doing so, as I think enough have been described for all practical purposes; certainly sufficient for the amateur to choose from to form a collection, no matter how large.

Such a list as the one here compiled, of kinds that are pretty generally met with at some time or other, may prove useful to the reader for reference in the case of doubtful sorts which he may come across, and, by whetting his memory, may enable him to distinguish one from another in cases of doubt. Therefore the list, although lengthy from a cultivator's point of view, may prove useful to some, as the descriptions of kinds are entirely from my own observation or experience.

I will now place the principal varieties in sections, in what I hope will be a useful form of classification.

OUT-DOOR CULTURE.—Black Hamburgh and White Frontignan.

GREENHOUSE OR CONSERVATORY CULTURE.—Black Hamburgh, White Frontignan, Madresfield Court, Foster's Seedling, and Alicante.

EARLY VINERY, TO RIPEN IN JUNE.—Black Hamburgh, Madresfield Court, and Foster's Seedling.

TO RIPEN IN AUGUST.—Black Hamburgh, Madresfield Court, Muscat of Alexandria, Buckland Sweetwater, Foster's Seedling, Trentham Black, and Muscat Hamburgh.

VARIETIES FOR LATE KEEPING.—Lady Downes, Gros Colman, Alicante, Mrs. Pince, Gros Guillaume, Alnwick Seedling, Trebbiano, all of which should be ripe by the end of September to keep well.

Muscat of Alexandria succeeds best when cultivated in a house by itself, although with extra care in maintaining more heat at certain stages of its growth it can be successfully managed in a mixed house.

CHAPTER VI.

PLANTING.

A POINT of the utmost importance to the after progress of the vines is their planting; and unless this part of the work is carried out in a proper manner, success cannot follow. To plant vines properly time is necessary to carry out the work efficiently, and to hurry over the operation means partial if not absolute failure. A little trouble is more than repaid by the superior crops of fruit which may be obtained, and in any case it is better to have a good crop than an inferior one.

I have already dealt with the making of the borders, in which, by this time, the soil will have settled down somewhere near its proper level, although settlement of the soil as the turf decays will go on for some time afterwards, though it will not be so rapid as at first.

There is no hard-and-fast line to follow as to the correct date when vines should be planted, and so long as the work is executed before the new shoots burst into leaf no harm is done; but for preference the month of February is the best where the border is inside the house, and thus wholly under control as regards heavy rains. Early in March would be better, perhaps, if the border be entirely outside and the stem has to be brought through the front of the house just under the sill-plate, as shown in Fig. 1. By that date there would not be so much likelihood of encountering severe frosts as a month earlier, and so much protection would not be required either for the stems or roots.

In any case, provision will have been made for covering up the border with some waterproof material to prevent its becoming sodden before the roots have had time to work in it, as this is one of the worst evils that can befall a new vine border, the soil at once becoming stagnant and sour. An outside border, even for the first year after planting, should not be left so uncovered continually that it is at the mercy of the weather, whatever it may be. It may be uncovered a few times during the summer, to admit sun to warm it and occasional showers to wet it, but a constant exposure to all rains assists the rapid decomposition of the turf—a thing to be avoided.

Presuming the border to be an inside one, that it is any time during the month of February, and that the soil has settled a little below the finished height which it is intended to be prior to planting the vines, more soil of the same kind as previously named should be added, treading the whole firmly down so as to leave a smooth surface—taking for granted, of course, that the soil is not wet, but just moist. To make very firm by treading upon it if in a wet state is a great mistake with a new vine border; as, instead of being left in a close, sodden condition, the soil should be just moist and no more when made firm, which renders it more porous when the time arrives for applying water freely to the roots; the idea in watering any vine border at any stage of growth or dormancy of the buds being that every particle of soil shall be made wet, and that the surplus water shall pass away as quickly as possible after it has performed its office. When the soil is rendered sodden and "cakey," as it is termed in garden phraseology, it is impossible that the water can escape as quickly as it should do.

The vines having been protected out of doors as advised in the chapter on Propagation, will be fairly moist at the roots, not wet or dry; but should they, through a heavy shower or from any other cause, have become soaking wet it would be well to place them under cover for a few days prior to planting, so that the soil about the roots will be moderately dry at planting time, in which state it is best they should be, as the process of disentangling the roots then is so much more easily carried out than when the soil is wet. The canes will be probably 6ft. long, or perhaps more, according to the manner of growth the last season; but for convenience in planting this length of stem may be reduced to 2ft. Turn out the plant from the pot, carefully removing the drainage from among the roots, disentangle these from the soil, and remove the whole of the latter very carefully—

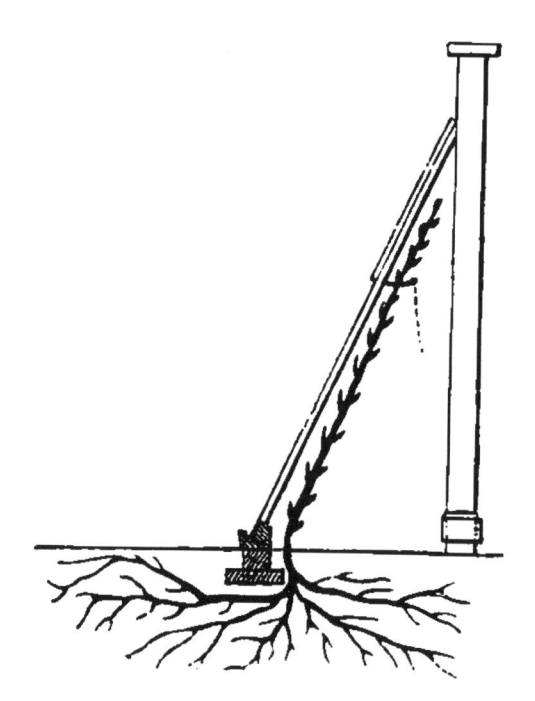

FIG 8. DISPOSITION OF ROOTS IN OUTSIDE AND INSIDE BORDERS.

a sharp-pointed stick is useful in doing this. Spread out the roots as thinly and as straight as possible on the surface of the soil as prepared. If inside the house, the roots should resemble those in Fig. 8, which shows them partly going inside and partly into the outside border, where the combination of borders is employed. But in the case of a border which is to be wholly inside, Fig. 9 clearly indicates how the roots should be spread out, so as to equalise them over the whole front of the border. For planting in a border entirely outside, follow Fig. 4, which represents the vinery with outside border only. The roots should be thinly covered with fine soil and about 2in. of coarser material over that, pressing it down firmly with the hand.

In three or four days, if the soil shows a tendency to become dry on the surface, give the whole a moderate soaking with water at a temperature of about 90deg. Afterwards cover it about 2in. thick with partly-decayed

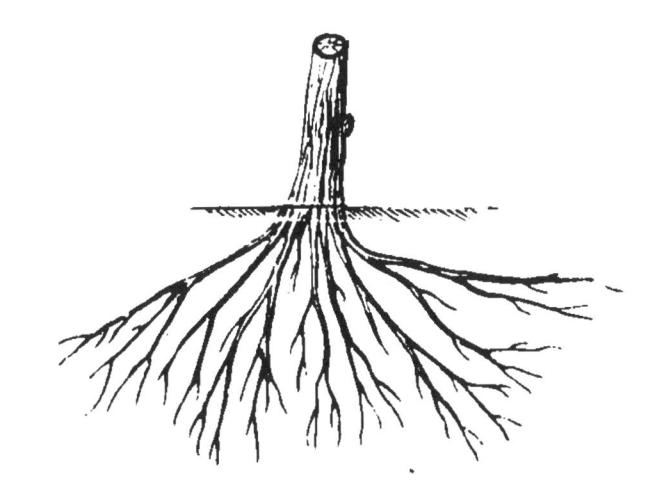

FIG. 9. DISPOSITION OF ROOTS CONFINED TO INSIDE BORDER.

horse-manure, but avoid treading on it when in a wet state. If it is necessary to stand upon the border, lay down boards to walk upon.

In the case of an outside border no water will be required, but the mulching of horse-manure is best applied at the time of planting the vines. Place a stake to each cane, to prevent it loosening the roots by moving about.

CHAPTER VII.

EARLY VINERY TREATMENT.

IN this chapter I propose to give the details of culture required by the early vines; that which is necessary for the growth of the Muscat and late varieties is given in separate chapters, thinking this manner of treating the subject will be more acceptable to the amateur than massing the whole together, as the difficulty of picking out the various stages of temperature requirements will not be nearly so puzzling where each is dealt with under a separate heading.

Early grapes may be had ripe in the month of April, but it is not probable that the amateur will aspire to any such high notions as this. What I will term his early vinery is one in which grapes are ripe by, say, the middle of June, which is fairly early, and quite as soon as they can be grown to produce grapes at all passable in point of quality. Fruit ripened earlier than this is very often produced upon pot vines (Fig. 10), which, although they do not give so good a crop as established vines do, are extremely useful where extra early grapes are needed; besides which, it is not necessary to occupy a house entirely with them, as pot vines can be cultivated along with other subjects which require about the same amount of heat.

To have grapes ripe by the middle of June, the vines must be started into activity and growth not later than the last week in December, that is, about the time when the vinery should be closed and subjected to the usual routine of temperature and other details of culture. Grapes to be ripe in June require six months to perfect the crop; those ripe towards the end of July do not take so long, as they obtain more sunshine during the earlier stages of growth. February 1st is soon enough for starting the vines to have the grapes ripe at the

FIG. 10. FRUITING POT VINE.

time named last, which would come under the heading of the Early Vinery.

The vines must have been treated as recommended under the head of Winter Treatment, which occupies a separate chapter. The house must be closed, admitting air at 65deg. during the daytime, and maintaining a night temperature of 45deg. These figures will be ample for a start, until some signs of life be manifest in the rods, by the pushing of the buds from the eyes. If the hot-water pipes be fitted with evaporating troughs, as they should be, they might be kept full of clean water.

The vines should be syringed twice daily, and a third time if the weather be bright and sunny; the first time about 9 a.m., then at 12 o'clock, and again at 2 p.m. when it has been found necessary to admit air to the house; it must then be closed, maintaining a moist, warm atmosphere. Three times, or even twice, each day, is too often to syringe the vines in dull sunless weather; once daily may be quite enough under such circumstances, and that time midday. The water used for syringing should be tepid, not less than 80deg.; the rods should be thoroughly drenched, not lightly sprinkled on one side only, but every part of the bark thoroughly saturated. The walls, paths, and borders should also be made moist at the same time; and if the hot-water pipes are warm, the steam arising from them will be advantageous in increasing the humidity of the atmosphere.

If the border be an inside one, or partly in and partly out, that inside the house should have a thorough soaking with water not less than 90deg. warm. When the shoots are ¼in. long, the temperature should be increased to 50deg. by night and 70deg. by day; these are the maximum figures, although the cultivator should not wait until the thermometer rises to 70deg. before air is admitted to the house at all, but the top ventilators should be opened an inch or so, so that the temperature of the house may rise gradually with the admission of air at the same time, which is a much better plan than allowing the temperature to rise to the maximum before giving air at all, which treatment is likely to cause a check to growth by the sudden rush of cold air to the inside of a heated house, which lowers the temperature too suddenly. If the weather be sufficiently wintry to require the hot-water pipes to be kept constantly warm to maintain the necessary heat, the borders near the pipes should also be kept constantly moist by sprinkling the surface frequently, as drought in any form is productive of insect life, which may prove most injurious later on when the foliage is developed. A dry atmosphere occasioned by a too sparing use of the water-pot is very often the cause of the foliage being attacked with red spider, an enemy which all grape-growers of experience endeavour to keep outside the house, because they know that it is impossible to perfect a crop of grapes if the leaves are infested with it.

The continuation of this chapter will come in that one devoted to what I propose to call Summer Treatment (Chapter XI.), as this will avoid a repetition of details, nearly the same treatment being required for all vineries throughout the summer.

CHAPTER VIII.

MUSCAT VINERY TREATMENT.

ALTHOUGH it is possible to grow good grapes of the Muscat class in a vinery of mixed sorts, yet, wherever it can be accomplished, it is advisable to devote a house entirely to this section, so that the treatment best suited to its growth may be accorded. It is an undoubted fact that the best crops of Muscat grapes are produced in vineries solely devoted to this kind alone. Although there are three or four kinds of white Muscats, one sort is quite sufficient, except it be for the sake of variety only. None of the various kinds of white grapes possessing Muscat flavour can equal the Alexandrian variety, which with ordinary good treatment will produce finer crops than any other kind. In the cultivation of this kind, more heat is required at stated periods of its growth than for any other kind of grape under cultivation, and in planting the vines this fact should be borne in mind, so that the necessary heat can be applied. It is while the vines are in bloom that more heat is essential to obtain a good "set," and without a sufficiency of heat success cannot be guaranteed.

Muscat grapes require also a longer period of growth than any other grape in cultivation, so long do they take to ripen. To have them ripe by the middle of August, the vines should not be started a day later than February 1st, and a fortnight earlier would be all the better, this allowing more time to put on that amber tint of colouring so pleasing in a bunch of this variety. The same treatment as regards syringing the vines, borders, and so forth, is applicable in the case of Muscats as noted in the previous chapter on the Early Vinery. The same night and day temperatures may be maintained also when the house is first closed; but as growth proceeds, the heat both by day and by night should be increased more rapidly, until the day temperature when the vines are in bloom should not fall below 80deg. with air admitted to the house at the same time.

The top ventilators should be opened a little when the temperature of the house is rising above 75deg., so as to dissipate some of the moisture contained in the house before the heat becomes too great for the welfare of the vines; and the sun shining upon the house too powerfully when the inside is in such a moist condition atmospherically is almost sure to result in scorching of the foliage of the vines, a circumstance to be avoided at all times and in any kind, but perhaps more especially in the case of Muscat of Alexandria, the foliage of which is probably more tender than any other variety.

The temperature during the day may rise to 90deg. with air in the house, gradually reducing the supply of air as the heat declines until the house is finally closed at about 83deg. The night temperature of the house should not fall below 70deg. certainly, and if it can be kept 5deg. warmer than the figure here named so much the better, to secure the perfect fertilisation of the flowers. In dull weather, when no aid is obtained from the sun in maintaining the necessary temperature, fire-heat must make up the loss of sun-heat, which should range from 75deg. to 80deg. during the day. When the berries are thoroughly set, and seem to be swelling evenly and rapidly, which they do if fertilisation has been perfect, the temperature at all times should be dropped about 5deg., as a continuation of too great a heat tends to weaken the vines in their growth; therefore, a gradual diminishing of temperature will prove advantageous to the vines.

When the bunches are in bloom, which can easily be seen by the bursting of the capsules of each bloom, displaying the flower perfect, each bunch should be sharply tapped at the stem, with a view to disperse the pollen on to the stigma, which assists the fertilisation of each berry. About midday is the best time for this operation to be performed, as then the pollen is thoroughly dry. Each bunch should also be gone over with a camel-hair brush, or, what is still better, a hare's or rabbit's tail fastened to a stick; by drawing this over each bunch, the pollen is thoroughly disturbed and dispersed.

The evaporating troughs should not be filled with water during the time the vines are in flower, neither should so much moisture be made in the house; the air should be dry and warm, although the sharp firing required to keep up the necessary temperature drys the surface of the border when the hot-water pipes are near to it, as they generally are. The surface of the border should be moistened over at least once daily during the time the vines are in bloom, to prevent red spider obtaining a footing on the foliage, which it often does, and in many cases the cause is a too dry atmosphere, a happy medium being what is desired in this respect. From the time the vines are in bloom until the grapes are ripe, the night temperature of the Muscat house should not fall below 70deg.

CHAPTER IX.

LATE VINERY TREATMENT.

FROM the point of view of the utilitarian, a good crop of late grapes is, perhaps, the most valuable of all, the fruit coming in at a time when there is but little else, excepting, of course, pears and apples, to supply the dessert. During the months of October, November, and December is the time I allude to, and praise the value of a good crop of late grapes.

Many cultivators, other than amateurs, make a mistake in late vinery treatment in this way. They do not start the vines into growth early enough in the year to secure a crop of well-ripened fruit which will hang in good condition until April or May if needs be, and they see early in October that the grapes are neither promising to colour nor ripen at all well. To make up for lost time at starting, they then have recourse to strong fire-heat to push on the ripening process; whereas the vines should have been started into growth by, say, the first week in March, instead of allowing them to break into growth in a natural manner early in April.

By starting the vines at the time I name, less fire-heat is required to maintain a steady growth, and this allows the vines to have the full benefit of whatever sun-heat there may be for ripening the crop in the month of September. All grapes which are intended to keep for six months afterwards should be ripe by that date. It is possible to maintain Lady Downes in a fresh condition until the following August, but to do this it is absolutely necessary that the fruit be thoroughly well ripened the autumn previous. Badly-ripened grapes do not keep well, as the skin is much too tender; neither do the berries obtain the right kind of flesh, or it is certainly not matured as is necessary.

From the foregoing remarks it will be seen that I attach a good deal of importance to the early starting of the vines to ensure a satisfactory crop of fruit.

Amongst the late sorts of grapes it is a very good plan to plant one vine of Black Hamburgh, which will succeed capitally in such a house under the same treatment as needed for late sorts. It often occurs, where two vineries are in existence, the one being devoted to early grapes and the other to late sorts, that there is a break in the supply of fruit during the months of August and September, the late varieties not being ready for use at this time. By planting one cane of Black Hamburgh the gap in the supply will be bridged over, for if the vines are started into growth in the early part of March, the Hamburgh will ripen its fruit at the time named.

The best kinds of late grapes are the following, ripening and being fit for use in the order here placed: Black Hamburgh, Mrs. Pince, Gros Colman, Alicante, and Lady Downes. The first for August and September, the second for October, Gros Colman and Alicante for November and December, and Lady Downes to bring in the New Year. It will be seen that the above are all black varieties, and this is simply because I consider them so much superior to any white variety ordinarily termed a late kind, always excepting, of course, Muscat of Alexandria. If a white kind is desired, Trebbiano is perhaps the best; it keeps well, and may be had in good condition at Christmas. A house 25ft. long will be sufficient for one vine each of the kinds here named, including the Trebbiano also.

When the vinery is closed, say on March 1st, more atmospheric moisture will be needed than in the case of the early or Muscat vineries, because the sun has so much more power, and the days being longer and warmer, moisture inside the house is so much sooner dissipated. The vines should be syringed twice daily, and oftener if need be, according to the outside atmospheric conditions, thoroughly well damping the borders, walls, and floor of the house at the same time. Previous to closing the house, the inside border should have a thorough soaking with water at a temperature of not less than 80deg. The night temperature may stand at 50deg., and that of the day at 65deg., to be gradually raised as growth progresses until 70deg. by night is reached during the time the vines are in bloom, allowing a substantial rise of 10deg. or 12deg. by day, with air admitted to the house.

The varieties named are free setters, and with the maintenance of a regular temperature night and day no trouble should be experienced in obtaining a perfect set of fruit. Lady Downes is the worst to manage in this respect, but plenty of heat during the time the bunches are in bloom, the pollen dispersed with a camel-hair brush, and the bunches sharply tapped about midday, will bring about the desired end.

During what is known as the stoning time is a critical period in the growth of Lady Downes, as without proper treatment at that time especially, the berries are liable to scald—that is, the skin on one side of the berries suddenly turns brown, as though boiling water had been poured over them—which not only disfigures the appearance of the bunch so affected, but renders the berries useless. An excess of moisture in the atmosphere, combined with an insufficiency of air admitted to the house early in the morning to dissipate the moisture before the sun has time to act upon the house, is the chief cause of "scalding"—the name it is generally known by. Those persons who are not addicted to early rising should allow the ventilators at the top of the house to be left open an inch or so all night, which will maintain the air of the house in a buoyant condition, especially if the hot-water pipes are made warm about the time when the stones in the berries are forming. A perfectly set and well-ripened bunch of the Lady Downes grapes is a good test of the ability of a person as a grape grower.

Late grapes require more water at the roots than any other kind, because the weather is hotter, as a rule, during the time all the growth is made; these varieties are also of a stronger nature, making more wood and foliage than other kinds, consequently needing more support. Especially free in leaf production is Alicante, the foliage being more dense upon this than upon any other kind, excepting perhaps Trebbiano, which is particularly robust in growth. Taken altogether, late varieties of grapes are easier to cultivate than any other kind, as no difficulty is experienced with the colouring of these sorts, especially Alicante and Lady Downes, given ordinarily regular treatment as to ventilation, watering, and so on.

Where the border is partly inside and partly out, provision should be made for covering that outside towards the end of September if the rainfall be considerable, as the grapes will keep so much better if the roots are not excessively soaked, which renders the soil colder than when it is maintained in a drier state. Wooden shutters made to fit over the border, with a fall to the front to carry off the water, are the best means of covering outside vine borders, as they are useful also to keep the border free from frost during the winter; but temporary coverings may be made of tarpaulins, old frame-lights, or anything else which shields the border from rain. The state of the border, be it wet or dry, has a material effect upon the keeping quality of the grapes, therefore any extra trouble taken in this respect will pay for the outlay.

CHAPTER X.

GREENHOUSE TREATMENT.

TO obtain a satisfactory crop of grapes from a greenhouse where a general assortment of plants are cultivated at the same time in connection with the vines, the amateur should content himself with few varieties, depending upon those that are certain of success, rather than upon those which are planted in such a house merely for the sake of variety. The chief factor in the production of greenhouse grapes, is the matter of admitting air to the vines. If a proper method of air-giving is practised, success can be assured; but if this detail is made a secondary consideration for the vines, then the chances are that the crop of grapes will be a poor one, and the crop of mildew upon the vines larger.

As a rule, vines which grow in the greenhouse obtain no fire-heat, as they are allowed to start into growth in a natural manner, and by the influence of sun-heat mainly. Commence by admitting air in small quantities early in the morning, always opening the ventilators at the top of the house first, and never allowing a draught to sweep through the house in cold or windy weather by opening the front ventilators at the same time as those at the top of the house are open. Only in fine weather, when there is no fear of draughts, should the ventilators be opened at both top and bottom of the house at the same time, before the grapes commence to colour; and especially should this be guarded against if the position is at all exposed to easterly winds. I have seen many crops of grapes spoilt by the attack of mildew on the foliage and bunches, caused by injudicious ventilation in the early stages of growth. The month of April, and often the early part of May also, is very treacherous; the sun shines brightly during the greater part of the day, raising the temperature of the house considerably in a very short time, while at the same time an extremely cold wind may be blowing from the north or east. At such times as these, the inexperienced cultivator opens the ventilators wide to keep down the temperature raised so suddenly by a powerful sun, thus letting in a strong current of cold air which sweeps through the house, to the detriment of the tender foliage and bunches, if they be formed. I have dwelt lengthily on this part of vine culture, knowing so well the harm caused by draughts of cold air, that the amateur cultivator may use considerable discretion in air-giving in greenhouse vine management.

Except in extra hot weather, the moisture arising from the watering of the plants in the house will be sufficient for the vines, as these will need attention at least twice daily. In bright weather the floor may be sprinkled at midday during the summer, but it will not be necessary at any other time. As a rule, vines in a greenhouse have their roots in an outside border, and require but little attention in watering, in some seasons none being needed beyond what the border receives from the rainfall of the district, which may be quite ample for the roots to perfect their crop of grapes. Should the weather be so dry that any misgivings arise in the mind of the cultivator, a thorough soaking should be given. If the berries are taking their second swelling after stoning, and about the time they are commencing to colour, liquid manure should be applied if available.

CHAPTER XI.

SUMMER TREATMENT, WATERING, VENTILATION, &c.

THE treatment required by vines during the summer renders daily attention to their wants necessary; and the success achieved by the grower will be in proportion to the attention given to small matters.

Watering.—This constitutes one of the most important details in connection with grape-growing, as upon its being carried out properly much of the success depends. Where vines are growing in a thoroughly prepared border, that is where the drainage is so arranged that stagnation cannot take place about the roots, it is impossible to give too much water to them at certain times of their growing season; but where the borders are not properly made, or the drainage is in an unsatisfactory state, there is a great risk in applying too much water, which tends to cause shanking of the berries —one of the worst evils which the vine is subject to; and although there are other causes to which the shanking of grapes is attributable, an excess of water caused by imperfect drainage is a certain cause of this defect in the crop of fruit.

We will suppose the vines are to be started into growth on a certain date by closing the house. The border inside the house should be well soaked with clear water at a temperature of about 60deg., giving sufficient to thoroughly wet every part. In the case of the Early or Muscat vinery, no more water, as a rule, will be required for the border in the way of a thorough soaking until after the vines have bloomed, set their bunches, and the berries taken their first swelling, as the water supplied to the surface of the border daily to maintain the necessary atmospheric moisture in the house will be sufficient; but late varieties of grapes, which carry more foliage and are started into growth fully a month later, when the sun possesses more power, will need the border-watering a second time before that named for the Early and Muscat vines. Just previous to the vines flowering is a suitable time for giving the second soaking of water to the border of the late house, and the water must be of the same temperature as previously noted.

When the bunches have set their blooms and the berries are seen to be swelling, say of the size of peas, then is the time when the vines need support. If they are more than two years old, a stimulant of some sort should be given to the roots. Liquid manure made from sheeps' droppings, or the drainings from the cow-houses or stables, is very good, used about the colour of brown brandy for safety. It is much better to err on the side of weakness than to give too strong a dose of any stimulant, as this has the effect of injuring the roots, thus causing a check to the growth, and this should be avoided in every form. When animal manures cannot be obtained artificial manures should be used, and these entail less labour in their use than do those first-named. Dissolved bones sprinkled on the surface of the border, just enough to thinly cover the soil, answers well, and so do many other manures which are specially prepared for vines, notably Thomson's Vine Manure. All that is necessary afterwards is to thoroughly soak the border with clear water, which carries the strength of the manure down to the roots.

If the soil which composes the border is inclined to be light and sandy in nature, another soaking of water just before the berries stone will be an advantage; but if the soil is of a heavy character, none will be required until after the berries have stoned, when they will commence to make their second swelling, and this is a good time to assist them by applying stimulative food, in the same manner as before.

The next period when water should be given in quantity is when the berries show signs of colouring; at that stage they swell very fast, and exhaust the moisture contained in the soil rapidly. In ten days or a fortnight from this period another soaking of water will be an advantage. This should carry the vines through until the grapes are ripe. If they are intended to hang upon the vines long, the borders must receive sufficient water to prevent the grapes shrivelling; the time and quantity required depending upon the weather, experience of the class of soil, and the depth of the border.

In the case of late grapes, during the months of October and November the borders may have a surface watering, which means that enough should be given to moisten the soil and roots near the top; more is not needed, as the roots lower in the border do not exhaust so much moisture after the grapes are ripe as they do during the time the berries are swelling and the growth is active. At this time of the year the waterings should take place only on fine bright days, missing it on all days that are dull and damp, so that atmospheric moisture will soon be dissipated by admitting air freely to the house, which cannot be done when the outside atmosphere is damp without a risk of causing the berries to decay —a circumstance which should be avoided by all available means.

If it is necessary to give water to the borders to prevent the berries from shrivelling, it is a good plan to cover the surface of the border about 3in. thick with clean straw, which not only retains the moisture in the border, but if put on directly the watering is done, the moisture from the soil is prevented from rising so freely, and thus causes less atmospheric moisture.

After the grapes are ripe, it is useless to apply stimulants when watering the borders except in the case of old vines; but liquid manure given occasionally to the roots of these during the season of rest will assist the vigour of the vines the following season. In all other cases clear water only is necessary after the period named.

When applying liquid manure or any other stimulant to the inside borders, the morning should be chosen for the work, as plenty of air can then be admitted to the house, and thus allow the ammonia which arises from the manure to escape. I have seen the tender foliage of vines burnt through not having the ventilators open when the liquid was applied. Excess of ammonia, too, will quickly discolour the paint on the woodwork inside the house if it is kept closed while the manure is being used. In all cases the water should be a few degrees warmer than the temperature of the house in which the vines are growing; and if, when the vines are in full growth, the water can be used at a temperature of from 80deg. to 90deg., so much the better. Copious supplies of warm liquid manure is just what vines revel in when in perfect health.

My remarks hitherto have applied to inside borders, for seldom indeed do the outside ones need water; but should there be an absence of rain over a long period, the vines be active in growth, and the border be highly situated and well drained, a good soaking of liquid manure would be advantageous, and in many cases quite necessary to sustain a heavy crop of fruit.

Ventilation.—It is very often a most troublesome matter to maintain the vinery temperature in a regular manner, although I am not one of those who think two or three degrees either too high or too low can make any difference in the growth of the vines; but I do not believe in the harmlessness of sudden fluctuations, night or day, to the extent of, say, 10deg., brought about by a careless system of ventilation or firing. Regularity in both matters is the correct plan to work by, I consider. The greatest harm is done by allowing the sun to raise the temperature in the morning to, say, 80deg. before any air at all is admitted, and then opening wide the ventilators, top and bottom, with a view to the rapid cooling of the house. It is such variations of temperature as would be caused by this that causes so much harm to the vines when in a free-growing state.

If a fixed temperature of 75deg. is required, the top ventilators should be opened a little when the thermometer reaches 70deg., increasing the supply of air to the house as the temperature advances; for both should travel together. If it is desired to keep the vinery at 75deg., the vines will not be harmed if the temperature runs up as high as 85deg. with plenty of air admitted; rather would they be so if the front ventilators were opened wide as well as those at the top on purpose to maintain a fixed temperature. Such treatment as this latter plan would involve could not do other than cause a check to the growth of the vines, even though it might not be apparent at the moment. In bright weather it is better to have the temperature a few degrees higher rather than attempt to lower it by exceptional means. Commence early to give air, increase it as the temperature progresses, and reduce both in the same manner, is the common-sense method of giving air to vines—or anything else, for the matter of that.

As stated in a former chapter, the early vinery temperature should be started at 45deg. by night and 65deg. by day, increasing it as growth proceeds until a night temperature of 72deg. is secured—this being at the time when the vines are in bloom. The day temperature at such a stage should not be under 85deg., with abundance of air at the same time.

The temperatures to be aimed at for the Muscat and Late vineries I gave in a former chapter; all that is required here on the same subject is to caution the cultivator once more as to the necessity of exercising care in adding and reducing the supply of air, which should be done so that the change is not at once perceptible but take effect in an easy manner.

Syringing the vines is of great assistance to them in promoting a healthy growth, if carried out judiciously; but to make a rule that the vines must be syringed so many times each day, irrespective of outside weather conditions, is calculated to do much harm to the growth. Syringing the vine rods with tepid water, to induce them to break freely into growth by softening the bark or covering through which the young growth has to push, is of much service, but should be discontinued directly the bunches can be discerned, or at least very soon afterwards. When the house is closed preparatory to starting the vines into growth, on every fine day the rods should be syringed twice, not simply just sprinkling them, but thoroughly wetting them all over. When the shoots are discernible the vines should not be syringed if the weather is dull or cold, and anything likely to cause a check should be avoided. The object of syringing the vines being to cause moisture about them, it is not necessary in dull or wet weather, as plenty of moisture is already present in the air.

From the time when the house is closed preparatory to starting the vines into growth, the evaporating-troughs on the pipes should be continuously full of water, with the exception of a brief space of time when the vines are in bloom. At that time they should be allowed to be dry, as moisture rising from the heated water would not agree with the pollen of the flowers, which at that period should be maintained in a dry state, so as to be properly dispersed with a view to procuring a perfect set of fruit. Excessive moisture about the bunches while they are in bloom has a tendency to cause the berries to be what is known as "rusted," when the tissues of the skin are injured to such an extent that they refuse to expand, leaving a brown mark on the skin, which eventually splits as the other part of the berry expands in size. All hot-water pipes should be fitted with evaporating-troughs, and if not so fitted, temporary ones should be adjusted, which is easily done. They can be made in the same shape as regular troughs, and zinc is perhaps the best material to use. The warm moisture arising from these troughs when the pipes are heated is beneficial to the growth of the vines, creating as it does a humid atmosphere, which does much to prevent the breeding and spread of insect pests, the worst of which is red-spider.

Manure.—After the berries have passed the stoning period, a little liquid manure poured into the evaporating-troughs with the water will be of considerable advantage, as the ammonia thrown off in consequence of its becoming heated is good for the foliage of the vines, as well as checking the ravages of red-spider, should any part of the vines have become infested with this pest.

From the time that the vines commence to grow in the spring the surface of the border should be kept continually mulched with a thin coating of manure of some kind. If the soil be light, cow-manure is best; if heavy soil is employed, then a thin dressing of partly decayed horse-manure is best. The object of the mulching is to encourage the spread of surface roots, for by maintaining the top of the border in a cool moist state the roots will remain and run on the top of the border; but if the soil on the surface is allowed to become dry and exposed to the sun and air, the roots cannot flourish in this state, but will descend lower in quest of moisture. Not more than 2in. thick should be laid on at once, and by continual watering of the surface and decay this thickness of manure gets less, and should be renewed as required.

In fine weather the surface of the border should be sprinkled twice daily, especially where the hot-water pipes are close to the soil, and the walls of the house and the pathways should also be moistened, as well as the vines syringed. After the syringing ceases, the sprinkling of the borders, &c., should be carried out, the idea being to supply atmospheric moisture, without which the vines cannot flourish, but insects of all descriptions will revel in a vinery where the air is dry and hot. A warm moist atmosphere is what vines rejoice in, and without it satisfactory progress is impossible.

CHAPTER XII.

FIRST YEAR'S GROWTH OF YOUNG VINES.

THE ultimate success of vines and the crop of grapes which they are destined to bear depend to a great extent upon the manner in which the growth of the young vines progresses, and the way in which the training of the shoots is carried out.

In the chapter devoted to Planting the Young Vines, we left them pruned to within about 2ft. of the base.

It is not wise to force the growth of these canes the first year by applying heat to the house; the growth should be allowed to commence in a natural manner, which will not take place until the early part of April, providing that only sufficient heat to keep out frost has been applied to the house during the winter. When it can be seen that the buds are swelling at the base of the vine as well as those near the point—the latter are sure to show signs of life first—all should be removed but two nearest the base. One only is required to furnish the ultimate rod, but it is wise to retain two as a safeguard in case of damage to one by slugs or from any other cause; for if one only were retained, the loss of that would cripple the cane for the year. When these two shoots reach from 4in. to 6in. long, they are pretty safe from slug attacks, as seldom do these pests attack them afterwards; but even then it is wise to take all precautionary measures for their safety, such as keeping the surface-soil about the vine sprinkled with soot. This should be done directly there are signs of life apparent in the buds, precaution being much better than the loss of a shoot. As a greater means of security against accident, directly the shoot is long enough to receive support, a small stake should be placed alongside, to which not only the main stem should be fastened, but the new growth as fast as it is made, for a very slight mishap might result in the loss of the whole shoot. The 2ft. of stem may remain denuded of its buds until the next autumn, as it is better to leave it than to prune away when growth is being made, bleeding at times being most difficult to check. When it can be seen that the lower growth is free and perfect, which can generally be determined at about 6in. long, the top shoot should be rubbed off, restricting the growth to one.

The soil about the surface of the roots should not be allowed to become very dry at any time after planting, but should be kept moist by sprinklings of water sufficient to maintain a moisture about the roots. Directly signs of growth are apparent in the buds, a moderate soaking of tepid water should be given, enough to wet the soil down to the depth of any of the roots, and deeper than that if any doubts exist in the mind of the cultivator as to its dampness. Although water applied to the border freely will not do any harm at this stage, if the drainage has been laid as previously directed, it is not well to maintain it in a too moist state, as that is liable to cause stagnation—a thing to be avoided; sufficient for the supply of the roots, and no more, is what is required. After the first watering, the daily sprinklings of the surface of the border will be sufficient until the roots have taken a thorough hold of the new soil, which will be seen by the manner in which growth progresses: the more foliage, the more roots are being made. Top and bottom growth goes hand in hand, and one cannot progress without the other.

From the time that the buds show signs of life the vines should be syringed in fine weather twice each day, early in the morning and again in the afternoon about 4 p.m., according to the time of year. Syringing the foliage vigorously helps to keep the vines in a state of healthy growth, and prevents the attack of red-spider or other insect life to which vines are liable. Be careful to have suitable water—soft is the best—and it should never be used at a less temperature than that of the house, but preferably in a tepid state, or one in which the thermometer will rise to 80deg. when applied. It is better to have the water a few degrees hotter than the reverse, because water applied to the foliage of vines when in a rapid-growing state at a temperature much lower than that in which they are growing is certain to produce unsatisfactory results, such as crippled growth of both leaves and stems, mildew, &c; in fact, such a check may be given to the growth of vines in this manner as cannot be recovered from in that year at least. Syringing in the morning should never be done later than half-past seven, and earlier by an hour would be better, the object being to have the foliage dry or nearly so before the sun strikes hot on the glass. In dull, sunless weather syringing must not be carried out at all, and the meteorological conditions should be taken into consideration at all times. In bright dry weather, for instance, the vines will enjoy plenty of internal moisture; but when the external atmosphere is damp and dull, the moisture inside must be reduced—these are the general lines to follow.

The result of too much atmospheric moisture will be apparent in the state of the foliage, for if this gets more than is good for it, wart-like excrescences will form on the under surface of the leaves, the points of the shoots will decay, and the leaves, instead of developing freely, will refuse to move beyond the initiatory stage. These are the first signs of excessive atmospheric moisture, consequent upon a too free use of the syringe and water-pot and the non-admission of fresh air in sufficient quantity to maintain the atmosphere in a sweet condition.

I have dealt at some length with this phase of the first year's requirements, as I know the ills resulting from bad treatment at this stage, not entirely through want of attention, but through unacquaintance with the requirements of the young vines, and therefore have thought it wise to point out the probable result of a too free use of moisture; for if I said, Syringe the vines twice daily, or even once, some amateurs might be led to follow this advice irrespective of the outdoor elements at the time.

When the vines are growing freely—say, about the middle of May—and the sun gains power on the surface of the inside border, a mulching of horse-manure 2in. thick may be used with advantage to the surface-roots, and the moisture which this creates on the top of the border will encourage the roots to run in that part of it; but if the border is left uncovered to the full force of the sun and air, it becomes quickly dry, and the roots go down into it in quest of moisture. If the soil is inclined to be light and sandy in character, a mulching of cow-manure will do no harm, if horse-manure is not available; the juices from the manure will wash down into the soil with the frequent syringings and waterings applied.

At no time must the vines lack moisture at the roots, and these should always be kept well supplied with water, which must be warmer than the temperature of the house itself. The same care is here necessary as in the case of the syringing of the foliage previously alluded to, and discretion must be used, it being most difficult to lay down absolute rules as to when the vines require watering in every locality. Towards the autumn, when the canes show signs of changing from green to brown in colour, which is the symptom of ripening, the water supply at the roots and to the foliage should be gradually withheld. The latter should cease altogether with the exception of a thorough drenching, say once a week, to remove any dust or probable spiders' nests from the leaves. This syringing is best done in the evening.

The manipulation of the shoots I have not yet alluded to, although it is an important phase; but I have treated rather lengthily upon the best manner to produce the shoots, to which I will now refer as clearly as possible.

We left the single shoot 1in. long, and this by the end of August should be at least 15ft., some vines growing 20ft. long the first year of planting; but if the amateur can produce a cane of 15ft. this will show that neglect has not been the rule, and that some good has resulted from my teaching. Encourage the leader to grow in an upright manner by securing it to the support until it reaches the wires, when the growth should be loosely secured to the regular wires of the house. It is not wise to attempt to bend the shoot suddenly close to the wires if it has made, say, a couple of feet growth since last attended to, because there is risk of injury resulting from such training of the growth, which is very succulent at this stage, and may snap off suddenly. This can be avoided by partly bending the shoot first, so as to get it into position for the next time of training. The main stem should be allowed to grow away at will; lateral growths will spring from each leaf, but these should be pinched off at the first joint, and again when they have made another leaf growth, which is called a sublateral; afterwards the growth should be restricted to this point. By allowing these lateral growths to extend at all, the main eyes situated at the base of each leaf will remain dormant; but sometimes these start into growth when the laterals which spring from beside them are removed entirely. These main eyes, for about 5ft. of the length of the stem, will be required for the next season to furnish growth for future use, or at least some of them; but how many will be determined when pruning takes place, and therefore it is important that they should not start into growth this year. When the leading shoot has made, say, 15ft. of growth, or a little less if the top of the house be reached sooner, the point should be removed, which will have the necessary effect of plumping up the buds near to the base of the vine. From this checking of the leader's growth extra shoots will start into life near the top of the vine where pinched, and three or four of these may be allowed to develop, provided there is space on the trellis for the shoots without crowding the foliage. Every leaf on the main shoots must have sufficient space to develop thoroughly; far better is it to have one shoot in this manner than a dozen crowded so that no part has enough space for complete development. All laterals resulting from the extending of the additional shoots consequent upon stopping the leader should be pinched off close rather than be allowed to overcrowd the rest. If there is plenty of space at command, the laterals may be allowed to extend one leaf.

The question of temperature is all that remains now to be considered in this somewhat lengthy chapter. Abundance of air should be allowed at all times when the outside elements admit of it; and this should always be admitted through the top ventilators, for it is not wise to open those at the front until the shoots have attained at least 3ft. of growth, and then but cautiously should air be admitted, avoiding at all times a direct draught, especially in the spring, when the sun has much power and is accompanied by cold easterly winds. Far better to increase the temperature by a few degrees inside the vinery than attempt to lower it by admitting air through the front ventilators. It is not absolutely necessary to use fire-heat to obtain a good growth the first year after planting, but if such a thing can be done the growth will be all the more satisfactory. A night temperature of 45deg. at the start and a day temperature of 65deg. will suffice, increasing it as growth proceeds, until during the middle of summer the day temperature may run up to 80deg. with air on, closing the house at that figure or two or three degrees less, when the temperature is on the decrease, syringing at that period. This is what is termed amongst gardeners "bottling up" sunshine, in which the vines revel; but it must be borne in mind that abundance of atmospheric moisture inside the house is necessary, as a dry parching heat is what vines object to, and is what quickly produces insect life in abundance, to the detriment of successful growth. The night temperature at this stage may fall down to 60deg. without doing any harm, but should not often go lower. In bright weather a chink of air admitted through the top ventilators at night will do much towards promoting a healthy growth.

As the wood commences to show signs of ripening, as

previously noted, more air should be admitted both night and day, until the ventilators may remain open altogether from about the middle of September until the leaves fall. At that time even the roots must not suffer for want of water, but should retain their freshness by being supplied with water whenever necessary.

I have not yet alluded to the outside border in this chapter. Where it is a combined one, or wholly outside, the winter covering should be so arranged that it can be removed and replaced at will when growth commences, to admit of the sun warming the soil, and it should be taken off altogether the first week in April. During the summer the surface should be kept mulched with manure to retain the moisture in the soil, but not so thick as to prevent its being warmed by the sun.

CHAPTER XIII.

MANIPULATION OF THE SHOOTS.

WHAT to do with the summer shoots is one of the most perplexing points in grape culture with which amateur cultivators have to deal. I have many times been asked to give advice upon the way in which the vines should be treated during the summer, and have generally found upon a visit to the vinery in, say, the month of May, that the whole growth made that season had been left quite undisturbed. All shoots which sprang from the spurs—and in many instances there were as many as four and six to each spur—had been allowed to grow and had reached the glass, a thickly-tangled mass of shoots, leaves, and bunches, scarcely penetrable by even a ray of light. I fear many vineries could be found in a similar plight, owing to want of knowledge on the part of the owner as to how the shoots should be managed in the earliest stages of growth.

To nothing is the old adage, "Put not off till to-morrow what can be done to-day," more applicable than to the duties which are indicated by the heading of this chapter. The management of the growth in the matter of stopping, tying, &c., should be performed directly the time arrives for it to be done, and, if possible, should not be put off until what is termed a more favourable opportunity. Favourable it may be to the cultivator, but not to the vine itself. Directly the shoots are ¼in. long disbudding should commence, if the shoots which spring from each spur number more than two. The weakest one should be rubbed off directly it can be clearly seen which of the two remaining growths promise the best, both in point of size of the bunch and vigour of the shoot. A little practice and attention given to noting the development of the shoots and bunches will quickly enable the cultivator to determine which shoot exhibits the best promise of fruit. When this is clear to the operator, the shoot showing the least promise, and, if possible, the one farthest from the main rod, should be selected for removal. The reason that the one nearest the rod should remain is that shoots at a distance from the main stem which are allowed to carry a bunch of grapes produce the eye to which the next pruning will take place, and the farther the shoot is from the stem the greater distance will the following year's growth be.

When vines are seen with very long spurs it generally denotes mismanagement in the manipulation of the shoots in disbudding, or is attributable to bad pruning during the winter. No vine should have the spurs nearer together than 1ft. on each side of the rod, and it is far better for the future crop and growth of the vine if a space of 18in. be given between one side shoot and the other on the same side of the main stem. The advantage of allowing this much space between the shoots or spurs is that it gives the foliage full opportunity to thoroughly develop. The main leaves on each shoot, especially those nearest to the base of growth, should not be crowded in the least, and each one should stand clear of its neighbour, for one fully-developed leaf is of more value to the vine than a dozen which are weakly owing to their being over-crowded.

When the shoots have made a growth of two leaves beyond the bunch, as shown by Fig. 11, the point of the shoot should be removed as indicated by the dotted line *a b* shown on the engraving. The stopping of the point of the shoot at the place named concentrates the energy of the branch into the bunch of fruit upon the shoot. Other growths will push from near the eyes on the same shoot at each leaf. All those between the bunch and the main stem should be removed, the easiest way to do this being to pinch them out with the finger and thumb directly they are seen; such growths are called laterals. Beyond the bunch the laterals should be pinched at the first leaf, and again in the same manner when another leaf is formed (*c d*) after the first stopping of the lateral beyond the first leaf. The entire removal of lateral growths

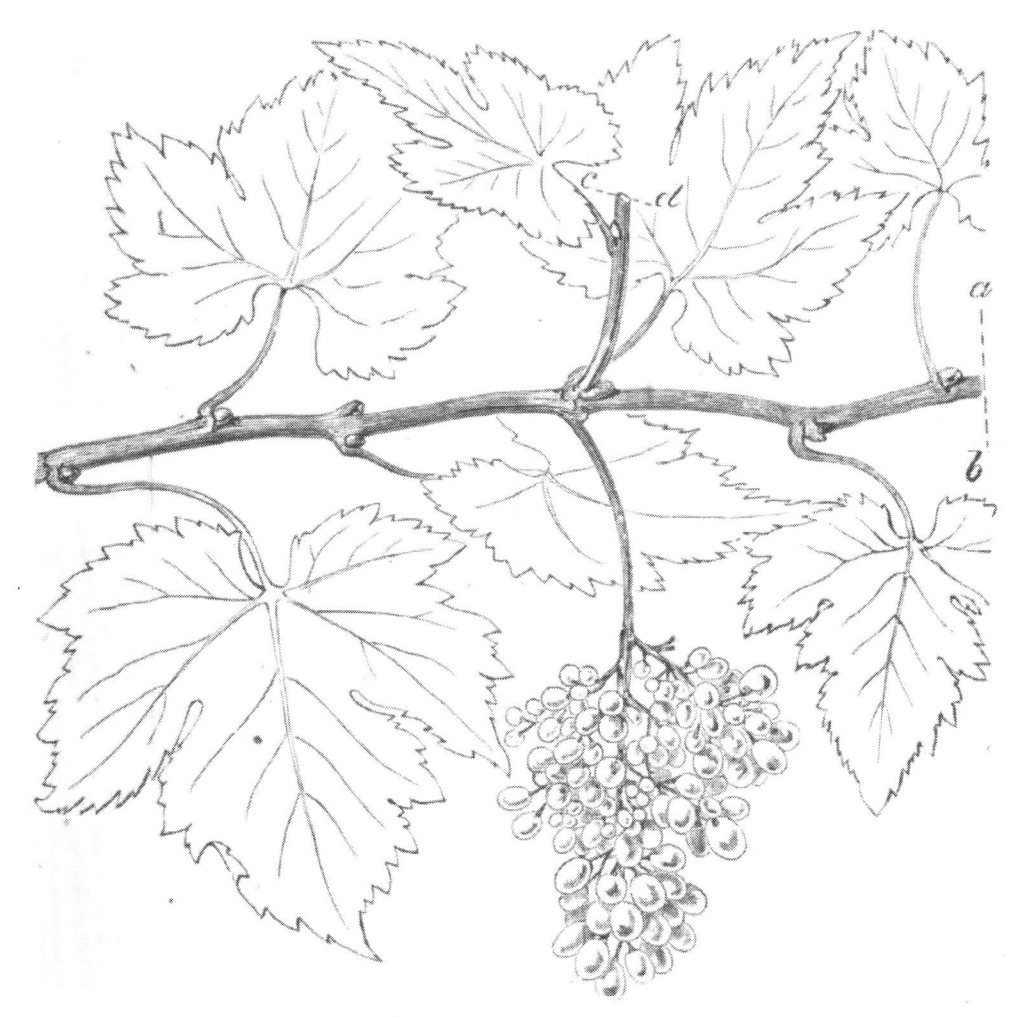

FIG. 11. METHOD OF STOPPING SHOOT.

up to the place from where the bunch forms prevents the crowding of the foliage.

When the berries are stoning they are at a standstill, so to speak, for at least three weeks, the formation of the stones preventing the berries swelling. While this is taking place it is usual to allow the lateral growths to extend a little

F

farther than at other times, with a view to exhausting he supplies in another direction, as the berries do not then require the same amount of nourishment as they do when the fruit is swelling rapidly.

When the points of the shoots have reached nearly to the glass, tying them down to the wires must be thought of. This detail requires some practice and judgment before the growths can be got into position, which is nearly horizontal from the main stem, with perhaps just a slight inclination upwards. Upon the number of shoots to a vine, and the position each is to occupy, depend whether they shall go in a direct line from the main stem, or how. In any case, the branches should be evenly spread over the wires, allowing to each as much space as is available, remembering that it is light which each shoot will be benefited by, rather than regularity in the placing.

When the vines are young the shoots are very brittle and most difficult to get down into position—i.e., each shoot laying close to the wires (on the upper side of them, of course, so that the bunches are supported). The shoots can only be got down to the wires by degrees, and sometimes it is not possible to bend them more than 1in. at a time, the danger being of breaking the shoot from the socket from which it springs. If this happens the crop of fruit (as far as that particular branch is concerned) is lost for that year, and perhaps the vine will be disfigured permanently, as sometimes other growths do not spring from this place to take that of the lost shoot. Often enough it happens that shoots left apparently safe, after being bent and tied down a little way in the evening, are found in the morning hanging from the wires by the support which secured them overnight, having "snapped off" when new growth was made, after some tension was put on to the shoot overnight. Proceed cautiously, then, with the bending of the shoots, for by degrees only can the bulk of the growths be got into position. Raffia grass is the best material for the purpose. In the case of the leader, continue to tie down the growth as it proceeds, stopping all lateral growths at the first joint.

CHAPTER XIV.

THINNING THE BUNCHES.

THIS detail of vine culture is of considerable importance, because on its careful performance depends the success of many crops of fruit which, left to themselves, would certainly be spoilt.

I have seen large numbers of otherwise good bunches of grapes ruined by imperfect thinning of the berries, or rather neglecting to thin them at all. Many amateurs do not realise the necessity of thinning the bunches, probably considering that all the grapes which are formed ought to come to maturity, and that they will do so without the trouble of their doing anything at all to assist nature in swelling the berries to a larger size than they would do if allowed to grow uninterruptedly from the time of flowering until the fruit should be ripe.

To enable the cultivator thoroughly to grasp the details of thinning the bunches and the reason for doing so, it is best to ask the question, Why should the bunches require thinning at all? The answer being: To obtain fruit superior to that which could be obtained without the thinning. To have grapes of large size it is necessary to remove quite one-third of the berries from every bunch, thus making space for the fruit remaining to swell to double the size it would attain if all were allowed to remain. A bunch of grapes, the berries of which were perfectly fertilised when in flower, has (as I stated before) one-third more berries than there is space for, and it is the cutting away of those for which there is no room that constitutes the art of thinning.

For the assistance of the cultivator I have prepared three engravings, showing the bunches in their various stages, and these I hope will be found helpful to the amateur in the operation.

Fig. 12. Bunch of Grapes before Thinning.

Fig. 12 shows a bunch of grapes before being thinned.

Fig. 13 shows a bunch just thinned, each berry having sufficient space to admit of its swelling to the fullest extent, according to the variety; and this is a consideration which must be studied, as some varieties require more space than others, on account of the great size of their berries. For

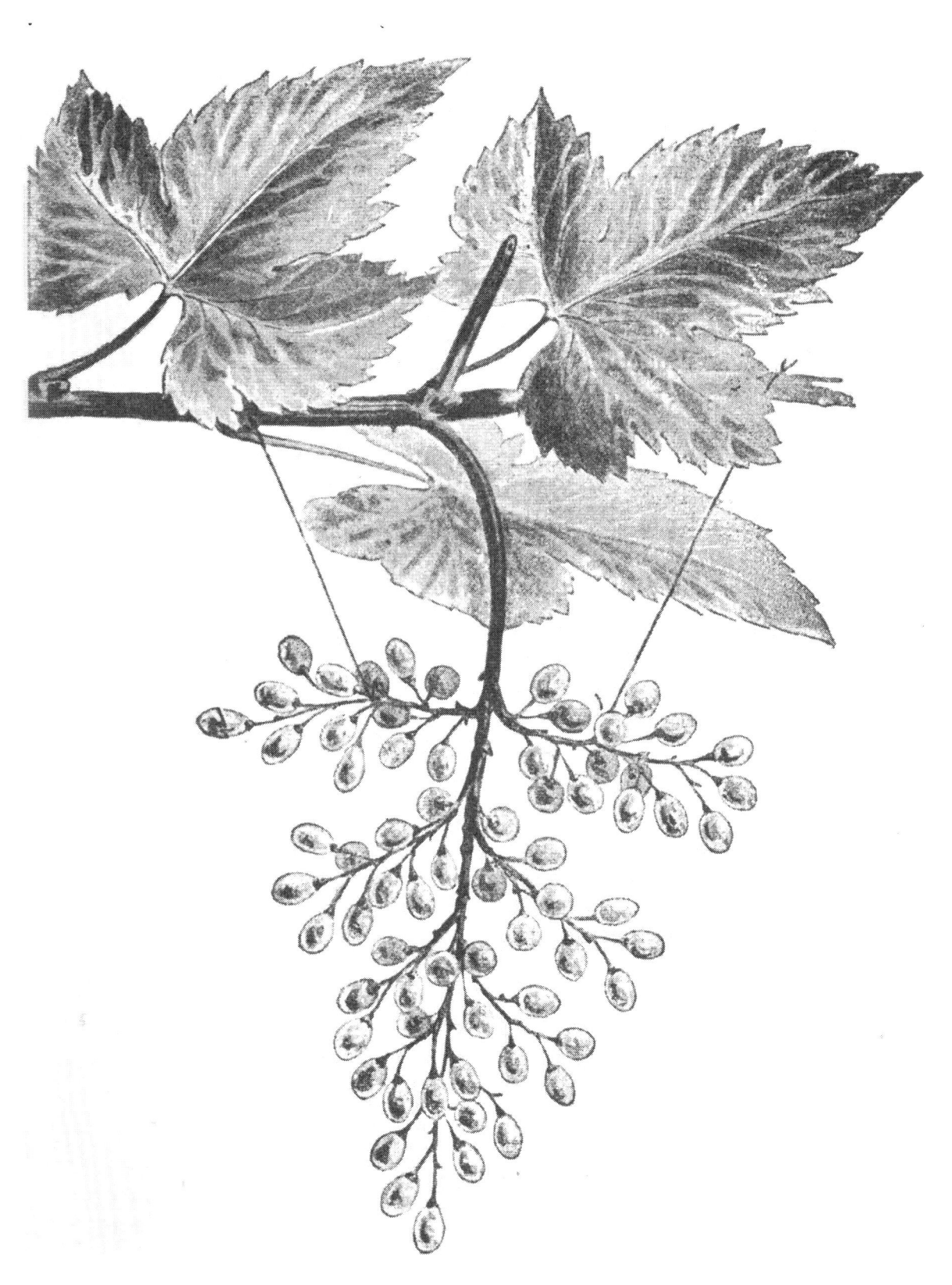

FIG. 13. PROPERLY-THINNED BUNCH OF GRAPES.

instance, Gros Colman will need more room between the berries than Mrs. Pince; the former being the largest-berried variety in existence, while the latter is one of the smallest.

Fig. 14 shows a bunch of Madresfield Court which has been properly thinned, allowing the berries to assume their proper size under good treatment. The illustration is not full size, being a reduction by photography of an actual bunch of grapes. The reduction was necessary by reason of the size of our page. From the engraving it will be seen that the berries are not crowded in any way, each having sufficient space, but no more, for it is almost as great an error to over-thin (*i.e.*, remove too many berries, so that those left cannot fill the space allotted to each) as not to thin at all; the result of it being a loss of weight of fruit and a loose appearance of the bunch, both when hanging on the vine and when cut. Indeed, over-thinned bunches present a very bad appearance on the dessert-dish, for, instead of standing up plump, the berries fall away the moment the bunch is laid down, owing to want of support, and the bloom is rubbed off by the berries falling one against the other, while every stalk is exposed to view, as well as any defects in culture, such as imperfectly-coloured berries. Perhaps there is no variety in the whole list of grapes more difficult to correctly thin than Madresfield Court. If the berries are left just thick enough, the bunches assume a perfect shape; but if made too thin, they exhibit a looseness which is detrimental to their appearance. On the other hand, if left too thick, the berries are more likely to split at a time when colouring commences; and this is the great fault of the variety, which to some extent limits its cultivation.

Fig. 15 shows a bunch of Black Hamburgh thinned in an imperfect manner, the berries being left much too thick, in consequence of which they did not attain full size, owing to want of space and being too heavy a crop for the vine to support.

Thus it can be seen at a glance what a thinned bunch is, what such work will produce when the grapes are ripe, and the results of imperfectly thinning.

FIG. 14. PROPERLY-THINNED BUNCH OF MADRESFIELD COURT
GRAPES MATURED (⅜ nat. size).

The first thing to do is to determine how many bunches each vine shall be allowed to carry, so that the crop of fruit will mature in a satisfactory manner; for it must be remembered that over-cropping is perhaps a more serious evil than any other single fault in the whole range of vine culture. Too heavy a crop of fruit produces the two worst evils a vine is liable to—shanking and non-colouring of the berries—and this to a much greater extent than many amateurs think, I fancy. The first year of bearing, one bunch of fruit is sufficient; the second year, three bunches will suffice, and so on until the vines attain the full size or length of rod they can extend to. In, say, ten years, if all other treatment has been right, the vines should be allowed to carry annually about fourteen bunches of fruit, averaging say 2lb. each, presuming the rafter space each vine can extend to is not less than 15ft. This applies to Black Hamburgh and Foster's Seedling; other sorts, with larger bunches, should carry a few less. If vines continue to perfect a crop of grapes to this extent for twenty or more years, little fault can be found with their management.

If the wood of the current season's growth is well matured, every eye at the base of the shoot will be thoroughly plump, as from these the next year's growth will spring, and from the shoots the crop of grapes will be taken. From every one, or nearly so, of these side-shoots two bunches of fruit will appear, and in some instances three and four will show, especially in the case of Muscat of Alexandria and Black Hamburgh. Directly the best bunch on each shoot can be determined—that is, of the best size and shape, most regular shoulders, and with tapering point—all others should be removed at once, so that the whole energy of the vine may be concentrated into the bunches remaining. Some cultivators allow these extra bunches to remain until the berries are set and ready for thinning, but this weakens the vines to a great extent and diminishes the prospect of gathering the finest of fruit; for there is a much greater likelihood of the berries not setting nearly so free—especially in the case of Muscats. When two or three bunches are allowed to remain on the same shoot, I invariably cut off surplus bunches directly their form can be determined. The time to commence

FIG. 15. IMPERFECTLY-THINNED BUNCH OF BLACK HAMBURGH GRAPES (½ nat. size).

thinning a bunch of grapes is directly the berries are set and commencing to swell freely—say when about the size of peas; in fact, directly the berries are seen to be perfect in shape.

Some judgment is necessary to determine the amount of space the berries of each variety require to grow to their fullest extent, and this can only be obtained by experience. Indeed, some varieties need more space in one locality than they do in another, owing to the suitableness or otherwise of the soil to their requirements—one variety will grow so much more vigorously in one part of the country than it will in another. Under no circumstances should the berries be handled or rubbed with the hair of the operator's head, because either will leave a mark upon them and the bloom will be removed, at once spoiling the appearance of any bunch and perhaps producing rust on the skin of the berries, this preventing them from swelling to their natural size.

It is necessary for the thinner to use a clean pair of vine-scissors, which are readily purchased from any nurseryman or seedsman, and a thin piece of builder's lath, 8in. long and ¼in. wide at one end, in which should be cut a notch resembling the figure V, this space being to support any part of the bunch, such as a shoulder, when holding it up for the purpose of more readily inspecting and removing useless and badly-placed berries; the opposite end should taper to a point, as this can be more easily thrust into the centre of the bunch than the blunt end. To support the shoulders of the bunches after thinning so as to give space for the berries to swell to their fullest extent some persons use small pieces of lath about 3in. long and ⅛in. wide, cut in V shape at each end: one end fits on to the main stem of the bunch, and the other supports the shoulder; but these slips of wood are at times rather difficult to insert without causing injury to the berries by rubbing them. The best plan, however, of supporting the shoulders is by looping them up to the wires one at a time, taking care not to raise them above the horizontal position, which would temporarily check the free flow of sap to this part of the bunch. Supporting the shoulders not only improves the size and appearance of the grapes, but it adds to their keeping qualities, by allowing more space for a free air circulation, which is one of the main preventatives of damping of the berries during the winter or dull weather at other seasons. Thin strips of bast neatly twisted is the best material for tying them up, one end being fastened to the shoulder and the other end secured to the wire trellis or branch which happens to be nearest.

Commence to thin the bunch at the point, first cutting out with the points of the scissors all small or stoneless berries, the aim being to retain only such as promise to swell evenly together, which alone renders a bunch of grapes perfect. As a rule, the point berry on each part or branch of a bunch should be left. In the case of Black Hamburgh, these little branchlets consist of three berries at the point, and the end or centre one should be left, cutting out that on each side. No berry should rub against its neighbour at this stage, and every one should have a clear space to swell in. The top or shoulder part of the bunch should not be made so thin as the point of the bunch, because more space is allowed for the berries near the main stem where it joins on to the shoot. A thinner who has had some experience can tell at a glance by the foot-stalks which berries will swell the larger: those foot-stalks which appear weak and bend by the weight of the young berries will not carry good berries, it often being found later on that these, having been imperfectly fertilised, are stoneless, and in consequence unable to swell to their natural size. The stalks which appear rough and strong are those which carry the finest berries, and these of course should be left, giving the necessary amount of space to each for all to attain their full size.

Those who have had much experience in any one locality can thin a bunch of grapes in such a manner that a second thinning is not at all necessary; but those who are only beginners should not risk the spoiling of a bunch by attempting to thin it finally the first time.

The bunches should be gone over once again when the berries are commencing their second swelling and just before colouring commences. Even greater care than at the first thinning is then necessary to prevent the berries being marked, even by the scissors, because at that time the bloom on the skin of the berries is fully developed, and the slightest mark at this stage will show more plainly when the colouring of the fruit is complete. Any berries which do not promise to swell evenly and large should be cut away at the second time of thinning. In many cases but few berries will need removing, though there are generally some in the middle of the bunch, where there is a greater likelihood of their becoming wedged, this close packing causing the berries to be much more liable to decay; and in the case of late-keeping varieties— Alicante, for instance, which sets so freely and is so thick in the middle of the bunch, needs extra attention in this respect—they should all be thinned with a freer hand than early or mid-season ones, as to maintain their keeping qualities the bunches require more space for air to circulate freely during the dull wintry weather through which they must hang.

CHAPTER XV.

INSECT PESTS AND DISEASES.

CULTIVATORS of grapes have many insect pests to contend with before the crop of fruit is gathered, especially if the details of culture are not carried out regularly and properly. Healthy vines are never troubled with insect pests nearly as much as those which are neglected; for instance, a lack of moisture both at the roots and in the atmosphere will quickly produce a crop of red spider, while carelessness in allowing plants that are unclean to come in contact with the foliage of the vines will very soon be the means of stocking the latter with mealy bug, perhaps the worst of all pests. Thus it will be seen that much of the trouble caused to the vine-grower by insect life is due to carelessness on the part of the cultivator himself.

Knowing well the evils attendant on the attacks of insect life of various kinds and of diseases (as I prefer to call them), and the difficulty experienced not only in getting rid of them, but in completing the ripening of the crop of fruit under such conditions, I will endeavour to point out as clearly as I can the causes, results, and best means of ridding the vines of the evils with which they are afflicted.

Red Spider (*Tetranychus telarius*), of which greatly-enlarged views are shown at Fig. 16, is perhaps the commonest of insect pests to which vines are liable. Vines that are once thoroughly infested with this small spider often require two or three seasons' careful handling before they can be called clean. The time when it is first noticed is generally between the time the bunches are thinned and before the berries commence to colour. The first symptom of the presence of this pest is that the leaves nearest the stem gradually change colour in the centre, commencing nearest to the leaf stalk. In looking at the leaves from the under-side through towards the glass they appear to be of a rusty colour, which gradually changes

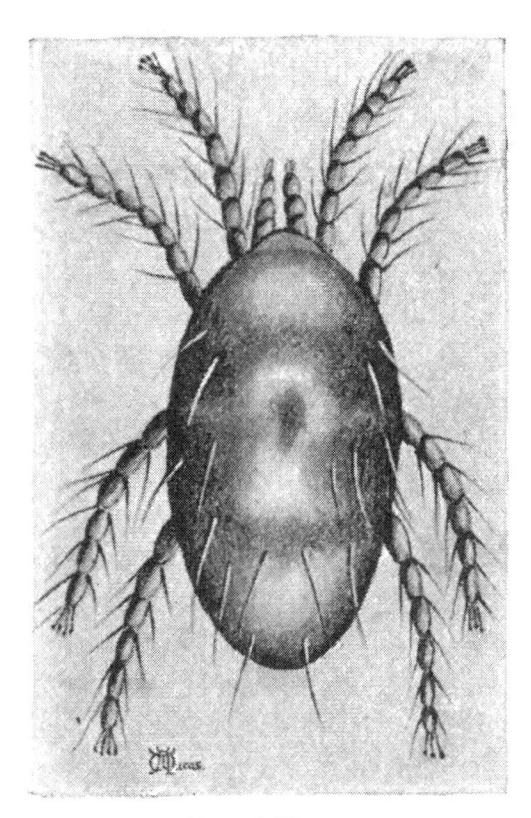

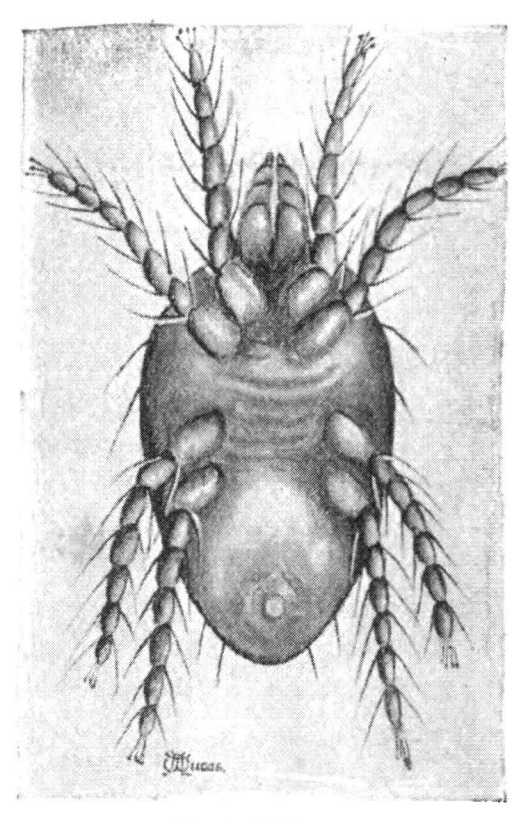

Dorsal View.   Ventral View.

FIG. 16. RED SPIDER (TETRANYCHUS TELARIUS), magnified about 130 diameters.

to a dull red, spreading all over the under-side; and if not checked the leaf will soon be covered with minute cobwebs. The leaves which I have named as being first subjected to such attacks are the most important to the vine, being those from which the vines draw some of their supplies of food; and they also, being nearest to the main stem, have an effect upon the next season's crop of fruit. Vines which do not perfect the basal eyes of the side shoots fail to show good crops of fruit from these eyes, and it is from them mainly that the next season's crop is expected. Therefore there is a double reason why the ravages of red spider should be checked before much harm is done to the leaves named. If it attacks the vines before the berries commence to colour, and is not checked at once, it is impossible for the vines to finish the crop of fruit in a satisfactory manner.

When the red spider is not introduced to the vines by the growth of other plants in the same house which are addicted to this pest, such as French beans or strawberries, and from which the spider manages to crawl on to the vine leaves, it is then caused by a too hot and dry atmosphere, and an insufficiency of water at the roots. This latter defect in the cultural details will produce a crop of spider in spite of the atmosphere of the house being kept moist. Attacks of red spider frequently occur where the vines are kept growing over and close to pipes which are constantly kept hot, especially if the vines are started into growth early in the year, more heat then being required to maintain the necessary temperature. This constant heat from the pipes to the one place has a decided tendency to dry the atmosphere in that particular spot, thus causing the introduction of red spider.

Some growers sponge the affected leaves with soapy water or tobacco-juice, but I have not much faith in this plan, as the remedy generally is only partly successful, and there is also a risk of disfiguring the berries in the operation, which, of course, would spoil them for exhibition purposes. Another remedy is to vigorously syringe the foliage with clear water every evening for a time; but although this plan would check the spread of the spider, the bunches would be spoiled in appearance. The water on the berries disturbs the bloom, making them unpresentable for the exhibition table. Some growers make the hot-water pipes as hot as possible, then cover them all over with sulphur and water made into a thick paint. The idea of this is that by making the pipes as hot as possible, the fumes of the sulphur are thrown off and fill the house, which is kept close, thus, as is supposed, suffocating the spider; but in the majority of cases this is only half effected. Often the cure is worse than the pest, as the foliage is burnt with the sulphur fumes, which seriously checks the vines.

I will now describe the remedy that I have found to be the most successful, not only in checking but in exterminating red spider. Upon the first sign of the presence of the pest on the under-side of the leaves, apply dry sulphur to the affected parts, either by sprinkling it on the leaves with the right hand while securely holding them with the left, or what is better still, by means of an ordinary indiarubber distributor. No more sulphur should be used than will cover the infested portions, or it may be shaken on to the bunches; but if this should happen, a few sharp puffs of breath will dislodge the sulphur without injuring the berries. Sulphur of a brown colour may be used; it is less conspicuous than the ordinary kind, and both are of about the same strength.

FIG. 17. THRIPS (Magnified).

I have dealt at some length with this pest, well knowing the evil caused by it if allowed to increase with impunity. Black grapes, such as Hamburgh, Madresfield Court, and Gros Colman, are perhaps more affected by its presence than other varieties. Rarely if ever do these kinds colour perfectly if the foliage is infested with red spider.

Thrips (Fig. 17), a species of *Thysanoptera*, is another insect pest to which vines are subject, especially Muscats. The small white or black insect, but most generally the former, causes sickly foliage, disfigures the bunches, and results in decay of the stems if not checked. The first appearance of thrips upon the vines is entirely due to the presence of plants in the vinery which are affected with this insect—azaleas, for instance. The best remedy is fumigating the house with tobacco smoke on three successive nights, which will generally be found to be effectual.

Mildew (*Oidium Tuckeri*) is a very troublesome fungus to deal with when once established in a vinery. The chief cause of its presence upon vines may be traced in most cases to draughts of cold air in the spring when the sun is powerful and the wind is blowing freely from the east or north-east. The heat of the sun in the latter part of April, for instance, raises the temperature of the house considerably in a short time, and air being admitted freely at both back and front causes a direct draught through the house, which in an exposed situation is very hurtful to the vines. A regular and careful system of ventilation will prevent attacks of mildew under the conditions that I have described. Another source of mildew is when the roots of the vines are in a cold, damp border and the temperature of the vinery is kept too high and close, not enough air being admitted to maintain a sweetened atmosphere.

I will now explain a remedy by which this fungus may be altogether eradicated in a season or two, even if the case be a bad one. Directly the first signs of mildew—very small mould-like specks — are apparent on the berries, the stalk of the bunch, or the upper surface of the leaves, vigorous measures must be adopted. The whole length of the main rod of the affected vine should be coated with sulphur made into the consistency of paint with clear water and applied with an ordinary paint-brush. The foliage, too, should have any mildewed surface sprinkled over with sulphur in a dry state. In very bad cases it is a wise plan to dust the bunches also with sulphur, even at a cost of spoiling the season's crop of fruit, but this may not take place. Sulphur can be removed from the bunches by vigorously syringing them with clear water, which will, of course, disfigure them for show purposes, but for home use the grapes may not be seriously affected. The hot-water pipes should be made hot and then coated over with sulphur made liquid with water, and dry sulphur should be sprinkled in any available places in the vinery. The idea is to thoroughly destroy the germs of the disease by the fumes. The atmosphere should be kept drier for a time until the mildew has ceased to spread. The following season a sharp look-out must be kept, as some slight attack of the pest is almost certain to be visible by the time the berries are thinned. The stems should be again painted with sulphur, in fact all the measures which were previously adopted should be again put into practice, with a view to thoroughly stamping out the disease for the future season's growth. In bad cases it is better to sacrifice the whole crop of fruit for one year than to only partially effect the destruction of the fungus.

Rust on the berries is generally the result of several conditions. In the first place a portion of the skin of the berries becomes rusted, so to speak, or in other words the skin is covered with a brown discolouration, which penetrates the skin in such a manner that the elasticity of its tissues in that particular place are injured; the berries in consequence cannot swell in that part, and as the other portions of the berries swell the side which is rusted cracks. Even were the berries not actually spoilt by the cracking of the skin, the bunch would suffer by the deformed and unequal size of the berries. The commonest cause of rust on the berries is the admission of cold currents of air to the vines when the inside of the house is heated. A sudden inrush of air in large quantities causes a chill to the skin of the berries, which results in rust. To make the case plainer, the temperature of the vinery is allowed to rise to, say, 80deg. without admitting any air at all: to lower this the ventilators are opened rather wide, cooling the vinery suddenly, and in a few minutes the damage is done. Thirdly, when thinning the bunches the operator allows the hair of his head to come in contact with the berries, which is almost sure to cause rust. At no time should the bunches be interfered with by either the clothing, the hands, or the hair of the operator, or rust will assuredly result. Rust is sometimes brought about, too, thus: The hot-water pipes have the previous year been coated over with sulphur to eradicate an attack of red spider; if this be not thoroughly washed off during the winter months, when the annual cleaning of the vinery takes place, the fumes arising from the sulphur, at a time when the bunches are in blossom, will cause rust upon the berries, owing to the injury caused to the flowers, when expanded, from the sulphur fumes. I have many times seen berries rusted in the manner named, and through no other cause than sulphur remaining on the pipes.

Warts on the under-side of the leaves is a disease caused mainly by the defective method of ventilation adopted. Small excrescences make their appearance near the leaf stem and gradually spread over the whole leaf if not checked. Insufficient ventilation and a too moist state of the atmosphere at the same time will bring about warts on the leaves. By lessening the supply of atmospheric moisture and admitting more air to the vinery a better state of the new leaves may be obtained, although those so affected cannot be altered for that present season; but additional growth can be made to assume a healthier appearance.

Scalding of the berries is very prevalent in some varieties, notably Lady Downes, and also, but in a lesser degree, Madresfield Court. What is meant by "scalding" is that quite one-half of some of the berries, every day almost, suddenly assume the appearance of being scalded with boiling water being poured on them. It most generally occurs when the berries are undergoing the stoning process, which is always a critical period in grape culture. The cause is generally understood to be the lack of a sufficiency of air about the bunches before the sun strikes upon them in the morning when the berries are covered with moisture, consequent upon an insufficiency of ventilation. Of course, such berries, when scalded, are totally useless, and should be removed at once, as no good can accrue from leaving them on the bunch. If the berries are attacked three or four mornings the bunches will assume a thin appearance, which disfigures them very much. The remedy is early ventilation of the vinery, thus dissipating the moisture which condenses on the berries before the sun has an opportunity of striking them.

CHAPTER XVI.

SHANKING.

THIS is perhaps the worst of all the evils which a grape-cultivator who has not had much experience has to contend with; though the disease is seldom thought of much consequence by persons having a wide experience of grape culture, if they are familiar with the vines—the manner in which they have been cropped, and the state of the border in which they are growing. These are important points to bear in mind, both by the cultivator who has experience of the particular vines, and by those who enter a vinery as strangers. Although shanking is but little known in some gardens, there is one variety which is specially liable to the disease, viz., that prince of grapes—Muscat of Alexandria. In the best of hands, this variety will sometimes persist in shanking, the reason for it being very perplexing and most difficult to deal with. In addition to the Muscat, the following are also subject to this evil: Black Hamburgh, Muscat Hamburgh, Trebbiano, and Gros Colman; and although other varieties will sometimes shank a little, it is seldom that they do so, except when the treatment is radically wrong.

As many amateur cultivators may not know what is meant by the term "shanking," however, I will describe the symptoms, and the result of vines being so attacked. The first sign of shanking is a small black speck on the stem of the berries, which gradually extends around the stalk, this in a short time turning quite black. It is generally the smallest berries which are first attacked. In cases of light shanking, only a few berries will be so affected; but in some instances whole shoulders, and occasionally even the whole bunch, will be spoilt, while the stem close to the branch turns black, and will shrivel if it is not removed. The berries are devoid of flesh, being nothing but water, extremely sour, and not in the least fit for use. It is at the period when the fruit is, or should be, changing colour, that shanking occurs; but of course berries so affected never colour properly, always remaining red, and they should be cut out immediately it can be seen that they are shanked. There are various reasons assigned for this disease, and these I will specify.

The most common cause, and certainly the surest way of causing a crop of grapes to shank, is over-cropping. Amateurs seldom appear to realise this fact. I have heard many express surprise that it should be necessary to remove any of the fruit which vines show in the initial stage of their growth; but it must be remembered that vines, like all other fruit trees, can only perfect a certain amount of fruit, and shanking is their method of resenting an attempt to exact an undue amount of produce from them. It will be seen, then, that I look upon over-cropping as the principal and most common cause of shanking,—a cause which all cultivators may easily avoid by being reasonable in their fruit requirements.

The next important cause of failure to perfect a crop of fruit is defective root action, which may be attributed to the borders being too deep, this inducing the roots to run at too great a distance from the surface of the border, and therefore causing many of the points of the quill-like roots to decay from excessive moisture, occasioned by the stagnation in the soil consequent on the great depth of the border, and it may be the defective manner in which it is drained. Again, if a quantity of rank manure be mixed annually with the soil in the border, or forms a considerable portion of the compost used in making it up, this will cause the berries to shank. The vines make such rapid growth through being stimulated and gorged, that, in addition to many of the roots dying during the winter in such a soil if the border becomes too wet or too dry, the wood so forced into growth does not mature sufficiently to perfect a crop of fruit. Vines which lose a great portion of their young roots during the winter have to make a fresh supply the following year; and as this cannot be done early in the season, a strain is put upon them, sufficient roots not being available to support them, and the result is the shanking of the berries.

A third, and also an important cause of the disease with which I am now dealing, is the sudden removal of a great quantity of young growth and foliage from the vines, the necessity for this being entirely due to allowing the shoots to grow and overcrowd each other before they are taken in hand, instead of stopping them at the proper time. Such a sudden check to growth as this involves cannot fail to be productive of evil. Regularity in dealing with the lateral growth of the vines when they are especially active is the best preventative of shanking occasioned by a too heavy defoliation; and some good grape-growers allow the lateral shoots to extend rather more than usual, just at the time when the berries are commencing to colour, as a means of preventing it, especially when there is the least suspicion that the vines are not as well furnished with surface roots as is desirable, perhaps owing to circumstances over which the cultivator has no control—such as previously formed borders, or inability to reconstruct them.

Vines badly attacked with red spider will sometimes shank their crop of fruit owing to the leaf tissues being so much injured that they are unable to supply the vines with the necessary food; and very often the disease will be produced by irregular attention to air-giving, or by a deficiency of fire-heat, occasioned sometimes by the discontinuance of its use altogether in the summer, when, a spell of cold wet weather perhaps setting in, and artificial heat still being unapplied, the air becomes cool and the temperature of the vinery falls far too low for the welfare of the vines. This and irregular air-giving will produce shanking of the berries, especially in the Black Hamburgh variety.

From the foregoing remarks it will be gathered that shanking is due to a variety of causes, all of which can be remedied by timely attention combined with a thorough realisation of what is necessary for the vines to perfect a crop of fruit; and I would impress upon all who wish to excel in grape culture the necessity of avoiding this disease, because, as remarked before, it is perhaps the greatest of all the evils the amateur has to contend with; for when it is present in a serious form the crop may be regarded as lost, and all the labour expended up to that date, and all subsequent attention, will avail little for that season. By attention to the different requirements of the vines, however, such as the making of the borders, the amount of fruit each vine shall carry, and the distribution of the growth and its manipulation, all the causes which produce shanking may be easily avoided.

CHAPTER XVII.

BOTTLING GRAPES.

GRAPES can be preserved for five months after being cut from the vines by bottling them, and indeed I have seen bunches of Lady Downes kept quite fresh and fit for exhibition after being in bottles for eight months, the show at which they were exhibited being held in the month of August, while the bunches had been cut early in the previous January. By cutting the grapes several advantages are gained; e.g., the inside of the vinery can be made use of for plants, which cannot well be done while the grapes are hanging, the moisture arising through watering the plants being detrimental to their firm keeping. Another advantage gained by cutting them is that the vines obtain a rest preparatory to starting into growth again. There is a certain strain upon the vines, even when they are apparently dormant, so long as the bunches are attached.

It is in the case of late varieties of grapes that the practice of bottling the bunches is most generally resorted to, although for convenience some growers cut part of their crop which ripens in August or September, and, storing them in a suitable place, keep them as well as if left upon the vines.

Although grapes will keep in good condition, as stated, for five months after being bottled, it should be understood that before bottling they must be perfectly ripened, as the skin of the berries is then tougher and less likely to decay afterwards, and the ripening should have taken place by the middle of October. Those bunches which have to ripen after that time—owing to the late period when the vines were started into growth or a lack of artificial warmth to finish them off in the autumn should the weather be excessively wet or be cold at night—do not keep so well as do those ripened by the time named. The best varieties for keeping are Lady Downes, Alicante, Gros Colman, Alnwick Seedling, and Muscat of Alexandria.

It is not necessary to have a grape-room erected for the purpose of storing bottled grapes only, as they can be kept very well in any suitable room; thorough dryness, darkness, and an equable temperature, of say 40deg. to 45deg., being essential, though perhaps it is not absolutely necessary for the room to be thoroughly darkened, as the grapes will keep quite fresh in an ordinary room. If, however, a room is set apart for them it will be better if it is darkened and kept close at the temperature named. The great mischief to guard against is damp, and if there is any suspicion of this being likely to be present, provision must be made to warm the room, so as to dissipate all moisture, although fire-heat is bad for the keeping of the fruit; and if the room is dry and can be kept at the right temperature without having recourse to artificial means, so much the better. Where a large number of bunches have to be dealt with it is necessary to have properly constructed racks with bottles to correspond, these latter being short with wide necks; but in the case of the amateur with but a few bunches, perhaps any ordinary wine bottle will suffice, and this can easily be hung up to a nail in the rafters of the roof, or elsewhere. If a piece of wire be fastened round the neck of the bottle (which should be filled with clean water) the weight of the bunch will balance the bottle when hung up, and in this way the grapes will hang clear of the bottle (see Fig. 18).

Any time after the leaves have fallen from the vines of their own accord the bunches may be cut, but about the first week in January is a very good time to bottle the grapes

90 GRAPE GROWING FOR AMATEURS.

which are intended to keep the longest, as the vines then obtain two months' rest. Three to six inches of stem should

FIG. 18. BOTTLING GRAPES.

be allowed to each shoot below the bunch, according to the distance of the bunch from the main rod. In cutting the stem upon which the bunch is borne, care should be taken not to interfere with the eyes nearest the stem of the vine, as these are intended to be left in pruning to give the next season's crop of fruit. This is the only point to be considered in determining the length of stem to cut in preparing for bottling the grapes. Where a choice of length of the shoots can be had, and the bottles in which the grapes are to be placed are not of a uniform size—and they need not be—it is better to allow 1ft. of stem in some instances, because it will be found that if the stem reaches to the bottom of the bottle the bunches will balance better when the bottles are suspended from the neck. That really is the main point to consider. A small quantity—say, one teaspoonful—of not too finely powdered charcoal in each bottle of water will assist in keeping the water sweet for the bunches that are intended to hang the longest; but for hanging say one month or so, this is not necessary.

When the bunches are cut, they should be carefully examined, to see that there are no decayed berries in the centre; and if there are any, they should be at once removed, or the berries nearest to them will decay also. Indeed, this point should not be lost sight of afterwards, and the bunches should be examined every week; for it is surprising how quickly one decaying berry will taint all those around it.

Should any of the bunches be infested with mealy-bug at the time of cutting, they should not be stowed away without cleaning, because at no time can they be cleaned so well as at this period. It is necessary for two persons to take part in the cleansing of any bunches affected in this way. One holds the bunch firm, the second vigorously syringes clean water into the parts affected, commencing at the top, as this has the effect of driving the bug from among the berries, it then falling off the points of the bunches. In bad cases it is sometimes necessary to raise the shoulders of the bunches with a small stick, so that the water may be the easier got into the affected parts. After the bunches have been thoroughly syringed, they must be hung up in the vinery for a time to get perfectly dry, which will not take long if the house is freely ventilated and the hot-water pipes warmed, a bright day being chosen to carry out the work.

After the bunches have been cut about two days, more water must be added to that in the bottles, as the stems will have absorbed a quantity, and any of these which were short may be quite dry on account of the absorption; but if the bottles be once again filled up after a lapse of two or three days, no more will be required afterwards.

The stems above the bunches should be left intact, as the berries are not then so liable to shrivel. Sometimes it is necessary to remove the point of the shoot, or even to place the stem in the water above the bunch, in consequence of the bunch being situated near to the stem or in an otherwise peculiar position. In that case, these bunches should be used first, as they are more likely to shrivel than those which have their shoots intact.

CHAPTER XVIII.

PRUNING.

PRUNING the vines is a detail of the utmost importance, and upon its proper execution depends the success of not only the following season's crop of fruit, but the appearance of the vines in years to come. There are two methods of pruning in vogue, viz., the spur and the long-rod systems. The former is the most generally practised, being the one which gives the least trouble to carry out year after year, and which has the best appearance in the vines. Scarcely any variety fails to carry a crop of fruit under this plan, and it is therefore much the best for amateurs. It consists of cutting back the current year's growth to within an eye or two of the base of the last growth. During the summer the growth is generally restricted to one shoot, unless in exceptional instances, such as when an extra shoot is required to fill up a gap, caused perhaps by an accident to one in the immediate neighbourhood, in which case there is no harm in allowing two shoots to grow from one spur. As a rule, though, one shoot only is allowed to grow from the spur, the side shoots or laterals pushing from the eyes above the bunch of fruit being kept pinched to one joint, although there are instances when more foliage is required to cover a certain space on the trellis than can be done with the usual one shoot lateral. Pruning back this side shoot to one or two eyes nearest the base is what is termed spur pruning, and whether the spurs will be kept short after say ten or fifteen years' cropping depends upon the manner in which this is carried out and upon the health of the vines generally; for if the growth is not satisfactory, the pruning cannot be carried out as it should be. The most important point to observe is to manage the vines in such a way that the leaf nearest the base of the yearling shoot is preserved intact during the growing season, for on the proper maturation of the bud caused by a perfect development of the leaf depends the next year's supply of fruit and the future appearance of the vines, because it is useless to prune to an eye which is not perfectly matured in the hope of its producing a creditable bunch of grapes the following season.

The long-rod system consists of having two or more rods to a vine, one of which is cut off annually, to make room for the next year's growth. This practice is sometimes carried out with old vines which have become exhausted by the long-continued practice of spur pruning, and which have new life infused into them, as it were, by running up a young rod or two every year. Black Hamburgh is a variety which succeeds well under this form of treatment. No lateral growths should be allowed to extend from the young canes, the growth being entirely restricted to the leading shoot. This starts from the base of the vines at the point where it had usually been pruned to before, whether on the long-rod or spur system. The shoot is trained straight up the trellis as far as it will extend, or say 10ft. or 12ft. long, and at pruning-time it is cut back to about 8ft. and cropped its entire length, if the number and size of the bunches be not too great; as by cropping the shoots their whole length, if they show fruit at every joint, there would possibly be too many bunches for the vines to carry and finish properly. It will be gathered, then, that under the long-rod system one year's growth is required for the canes to attain to maturity; and therefore it will be obvious that those who practise this system need to lay in a number of shoots annually to provide for a regular supply of fruit.

The time to prune the vines is the next consideration which interests us. At any time most convenient after the leaves fall the vines may be pruned; but as a rule, from the first week in November until the first week in January is the best time in which to carry out the work. If delayed much longer than the latter period, it sometimes happens that the vines will bleed considerably, as the sap is then rising preparatory to the buds starting into growth.

What is meant by "bleeding" is a loss of sap, which exudes through the freshly-cut parts of the shoots, and this cannot fail to weaken the vines for a time, at any rate. Some growers say that excessive bleeding in vines is caused by the wood not being properly ripened; but I have seen vines bleed extremely in spite of their being apparently thoroughly matured. This loss of sap goes on in spite of all attempts to stop it, until growth is so far advanced as to cause a cessation by assimilation.

The subject of pruning vines should be divided into two parts, as it is necessary to adopt a somewhat different system when dealing with established vines to that which is necessary in dealing with young plants. In the case of the latter especially, extreme care should be exercised, and a knowledge of how to proceed should be gained before undertaking the somewhat difficult task of pruning those that have not borne a crop of fruit, and those which have carried but a single one.

I think it will be most convenient to take the young vines first in describing the method to be adopted in the pruning. Assuming, then, that the vine started its growth from the base whence as a pot plant the first growth sprang. This would be on a level with the border, the growth having progressed up the trellis to the top of the house, or nearly so, for the first year—say to a length of 12 feet. We will also assume that the vines in question are expected to last in good condition for at least twenty years without renewal of the canes. A greater length of rod should not be allowed to remain at the first pruning than will provide one pair of side shoots and a leader, which means that the cane should be cut back to within three buds of the first wire, which is generally placed about 18in. or 2ft. from the border.

It is more than likely that one bunch of fruit will show on each side growth—and upon the leader also, for the matter of that—but it is never good policy to allow the leading growth of young vines to carry even one bunch of fruit. It is better for their future progress for their strength to be spent in growth rather than in perfecting fruit upon the leaders.

Some persons may wonder why young vines should not be allowed to carry more than two bunches at the most, which I recommend; indeed, I am strongly in favour of their only carrying one bunch the first year. The reason is, that by over-cropping them the first year, the growth becomes crippled and never regains the vigour necessary to last in good condition twenty years. Were they only intended to last five or six years at the most, it would not matter if they were allowed to carry half-a-dozen bunches the first year. No vine, then, should be allowed to carry more than two bunches of fruit if it is expected to exist the maximum number of years. These bunches can be had from the two side shoots. It is useless to prune to a longer length of cane, as this would weaken the vine rather than concentrate its energy into three shoots. I have seen many vines spoilt by mismanagement in this way.

The second year of pruning is of equal importance to the future welfare of the vine in the same respect.

Fig. 19 shows how to prune the vine the second year. The pair of side shoots left the year previous are cut back to within two eyes of the cane, or main rod, as it is now called. The reason for allowing two eyes on each side shoot is to give "two strings to the bow" in the matter of choice of bunches of fruit. If the basal leaf of the current year's growth does not come perfect in form and develop itself fully, there is not much likelihood of a good bunch of grapes coming from the eye in question; so that by leaving two buds a

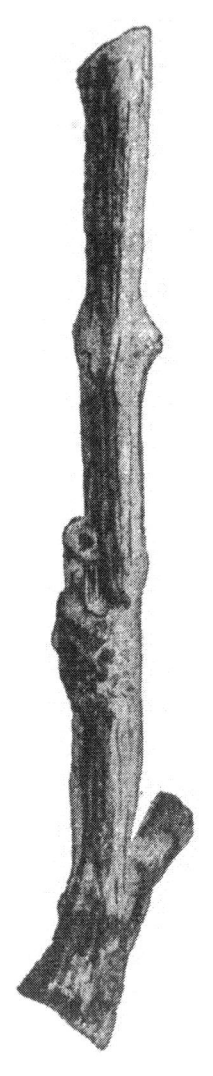

FIG. 19.
SECOND YEAR
OF PRUNING.

choice is obtained. The length of the leader should not be more than 2ft. for the second year, for the same reasons as stated previously. I have seen many vines spoilt from no other cause than mismanagement in pruning the second year as well as in the first. Some leave 6ft. of rod the first or second year, the idea being that the roof will the more quickly be covered and a full crop of fruit be the result in a shorter space of time. The consequence of this proceeding is that the eyes nearest the top break strongest and grow in the same way the whole season, the eyes nearest the base often refusing to start at all, while many of those in the middle of the cane grow very weak, and can be picked out ever after as the result of allowing too much length of leader.

Fig. 20 shows how to manipulate the lateral growths made on the leader, *a* denoting one shoot cut off and showing the dormant bud, from which will spring the shoot the following year. From this shoot a bunch may be taken, and it also lays the foundation of the future spur. *b*, with dotted lines across the shoot, shows a similar shoot to the last, but not cut off. It will be noticed that this shoot was stopped at the first joint, and that it formed another growth, which is termed a "sub-lateral"; this will be shortened in the autumn when the growth is becoming

FIG. 20. HOW TO PRUNE LEADER.

matured. If the amateur carefully observes the manner of cutting illustrated in this engraving, he ought not to find any difficulty in carrying out the pruning of his young vines in a satisfactory manner.

I will now give details of how established vines should be

treated on the short-spur system. With a sharp pruning-knife cut the shoots—last season's growth—to within two eyes or buds of the spur where the same shoot was cut the previous year. Two are left at pruning-time to allow of a choice being made if necessary, as sometimes a bunch of fruit does not show on every growth the following spring, and by leaving two eyes there is a double chance of fruit, while a choice can be made of the best bunch if two form; sometimes, also, an accident may occur to a single shoot or bud on the one spur. In this way a gap would be made in the rod. By practising what I will call the "double-bud" method, however, accidents are provided against somewhat. When each of the shoots resulting from the retention of two buds shows a bunch of fruit, the one farthest from the base of the rod is removed, in this manner reducing the length of the spur. It will be readily seen that if the shoot farthest from the vine were retained, the spur would in time become longer than if the eye nearest the rod were retained each year.

In pruning the vines a sharp knife should always be used, making short cuts in all cases; those made in a lengthy flat manner do not present such a neat appearance as those cut nearly square across. It is a good plan to apply a dressing of Thomson's Styptic to every cut; it is adhesive and quickly assumes a stiff glazed appearance, and generally has the effect of preventing the wounds from bleeding to any great extent. But vines which are well matured require nothing in the way of sealing the ends of the cut parts, although, as stated previously, some vines will persist in losing sap in a most unaccountable manner, and therefore I advise that the old adage, "prevention is better than cure," be borne in mind in this connection.

CHAPTER XIX.

WINTER TREATMENT.

MUCH is required to be done in the vinery during the winter months in the way of pruning the vines—a subject dealt with in the preceding chapter—cleaning them if necessary, and also the house itself; renovating the border on the surface, which will be a stimulus to growth during the coming season; and various other odd jobs, which all come under the head of winter treatment. Probably, though, many amateurs lack the knowledge of what to do, how to do it, and when to do it, so that a good crop of fruit for the next year may be produced.

Directly the leaves have fallen is the time to set about the winter treatment, as circumstances admit, such as a wet day or wintry weather, when operations in the outside garden cannot be got on with. The first thing to do is to prune the vines, getting rid of superfluous shoots, which only interfere with the thorough cleansing of the vines and vinery. The vines should then be removed from the wires and laid down on the border close to the front of the house, to be out of the way for the time being. The woodwork and glass should be thoroughly cleansed with hot water and soft soap, well scrubbing the wood with a hard brush to remove all dirt, and thoroughly working it into any crevices which are favourable to the safe hiding of mealy-bug or any other insect pest. The glass also should be made quite clean, which will be an assistance to the growth of the vines the following season by admitting more light to the foliage, as dirty glass is certainly a serious obstruction to light. The best method of cleaning the woodwork and iron is to apply a couple of coats of paint, which is not only the best preservative of the timber, but is also the best way to destroy all insect life.

When the roof has been made thoroughly clean, the next step is to cleanse the vines themselves. I do not hold with the barbarous practice of scraping off annually all the bark close to the wood; such skinning of the rods is against nature and cannot be productive of good results. In the case of vines affected with mealy-bug, the loose bark around the spurs especially should be rubbed off with the hand, as directed in the chapter devoted to Insect Pests, on page 77, the vines being washed as there recommended. If the vines were not affected by insects in the year previous, it will not be necessary to remove any of the bark from the stems, but simply to give the canes a scrubbing with hot water and soft soap, using a hard brush.

This washing is intended more as a means of preventing the spread of insect life than anything else, for one can never tell what pest is going to tackle the vines and give trouble the following season; therefore, any extra labour spent in the shape of cleanliness on the winter treatment will be of advantage to the future of the vines. Some persons recommend the stems to be coated over with a mixture of clay, soot, sulphur, &c., with a view to kill insect life, but I fail to see the efficacy of such treatment, as none of the ingredients named are fatal to insect life, and it only covers them up while in a dormant state; the mixture afterwards becoming dry, cracks, and out come the pests which were supposed to be killed. I have tried many of these reputed remedies, but do not believe that any of them are of service. Clean hot water and soft soap, if properly applied, will do more towards killing insect life than anything else.

When the vines have been thoroughly cleaned, it is usual to tie them down to the wires along the front of the vinery, bending one across the other; the reason for doing this being that they are then out of the way in case the vinery has to be used for plants as well. They are also easier to syringe when the time comes for that to be done, because they are more in a mass and occupy less space than when spread over the whole under-side of the roof. The next is perhaps the most important reason of all for tying the vines in a downward direction. When the eyes start into life in due season, it is found that they break more regularly into growth, owing to the flow of sap to the leading eyes being checked. The shoots near the base are as quick in their growth as those near the top of the rod; and it is advisable to have all the shoots on the rods of the same age, because if the bunches are in bloom on one part of the vines and those on the points are somewhat later, the temperature required for those in the blooming stage will not agree with the others.

The walls of the vinery, back and front, also the pillars which support the pipes, will next need attention. As a rule, these are lime-washed, and in some cases painted; but I do not think there is a better plan than the former, as lime has a sweetening effect wherever used. All parts should be thoroughly gone over, well filling the crevices, and applying the lime in a hot state, quite fresh and unslaked.

The hot-water pipes should have an annual coat of lamp-black and boiled oil, which is much the best mixture for the purpose, as it does not interfere with the radiation of heat from the pipes, as is the case with paint or black varnish, for instance. If the pipes are treated in the manner indicated, their appearance will be much improved. Another advantage attending the coating of the pipes is that it thoroughly cleanses them from any sulphur applied to them during the previous summer for cleansing the foliage of red spider. Any sulphur left now is liable to cause rust to the berries.

The surface of the border will next claim attention. All the loose soil and dry exhausted manure, the result of the previous mulching, should be removed, as no advantage is gained by allowing it to remain longer. The loose surface-soil should be removed as far down as to disclose the roots; a dressing 2in.

thick, should then be laid on the surface of the border, this dressing consisting of fresh-cut turf chopped into pieces about 2in. square, mixed with a small portion of bone-meal or some other fertiliser—such as Thomson's Vine Manure, following the instructions given with it regarding the quantity to use. If the soil is inclined to be of a heavy character, add some wood ashes, charcoal, or old mortar, about one-quarter of a bushel to each fair-sized wheelbarrow-load of soil. Do not previously fork over the surface of the border, or otherwise interfere with the roots. Some persons think it is necessary to dig the border, but such work is a mistake, as it cannot be done without causing considerable injury to the roots by breaking them with the fork. The soil used for the top-dressing should be in a moist state, neither too wet nor too dry. Tread it down firmly, and cover it with a 2in. covering of manure from the stables, consisting mainly of the fresh droppings. This kind of manure is especially to be recommended for vines where the soil is of a heavy character, as it is light and contains much ammonia. In the case of light sandy soil, cow-manure is best. These mulchings of the surface with suitable manures are of considerable benefit to the vines, increasing the surface roots very rapidly when the vines are in good health and the roots are near to the surface, as they should be in all borders; they also maintain the surface of the border in a moist state during the hot weather in summer, and therefore encourage root action, which cannot be the case if the soil is dry about the roots, for they will then travel in search of moisture downwards if they cannot obtain it near the surface.

In some districts the soil is deficient in lime, an ingredient which is necessary for the growth of vines in the best condition. If lime is not naturally in the soil, and one does not expect to find it in a sandy soil, some must be added. The best time to apply this is when top-dressing the border during the winter. Instead of quite baring the roots, leave enough soil to cover them, removing all coarse particles of manure which have become exhausted, and consequently of no value. Cover the border entirely over with lime which has not been slaked, but kept in a fresh and quick state; over the lime lay the soil, as previously directed, and the manure mulching as well. If the lime be laid on ½in. thick, it will not be too much.

Throughout the winter months, when the vines are at rest, the soil in the border must not be allowed to become dry, but be kept in a moist state by frequent applications of water to the surface, if not required right through the border, or the roots will shrivel and lose their use in conveying nutriment to the vines, even though the canes be in a dormant state. It is neglect of this detail which is often the cause of a lack of surface roots, as these cannot exist in a dry parched soil, and consequently vanish, much to the detriment of the vines themselves — the surface roots being one of their main supports.

If the soil for the top-dressing cannot be obtained in any other than a wet state, it should not be trodden upon for a time, until it has had an opportunity of drying a little, or it will become heavy and sodden, in which state the roots will not enter it freely, neither can subsequent waterings be properly given, as water cannot percolate through the soil, and consequently the lower part of the border remains in a dry state when it is thought to be moist enough, judging by the appearance of the surface. This, by the way, is a fallacious means of determining whether the whole depth of border needs water or not. A much better plan, if doubt exists in the mind of the cultivator about the state of the border, is to dig down to its depth and ascertain its state. Should it be necessary to walk upon the border after top-dressing it, lay some boards down to walk upon, as this prevents the soil running together in an inert mass.

CHAPTER XX.

INARCHING VINES.

INARCHING is a convenient method of substituting one variety of grape for another in the same house without going to the trouble of entirely removing the vine objected to, perhaps because it is not suitable for the purpose required, or is of inferior quality, a bad setter, or of short keeping capability.

It is a well-known fact amongst grape-growers that young vines planted in an old border hardly ever make satisfactory progress, and therefore the best plan is to inarch a desirable kind on to that which is not so. Fig. 21 represents a vine inarched on to an existing plant. The best time for the operation is when both stock and scion are in a growing state, as the union does not take place when the sap is dormant. Presuming that a vinery is started into growth about the first week in February, or a month later even, any time towards the end of April (or the same time in May for the vines last started) will be suitable for the purpose of inarching. The plant to be united to the existing stock must be in a movable condition—*i.e.*, growing in a pot—so that it can be placed in close proximity to the stock to be operated upon. It matters little where the union is made on the existing vine, as far as the actual process of inarching is concerned; but where the new sort is to take the place of the older and rejected variety, it is well to start the new kind near to the base of the old vine. A position about the first wire or close to the first set of spurs is a good site to make the union, because then the new variety derives the full benefit for cropping purposes of the entire length of the rafters, in the same way as the previous kind did.

When the vine in the pot has made, say 1ft. of growth, and the bark has become fairly hard, then it may be assumed that it is in a fair condition for operation. The number of

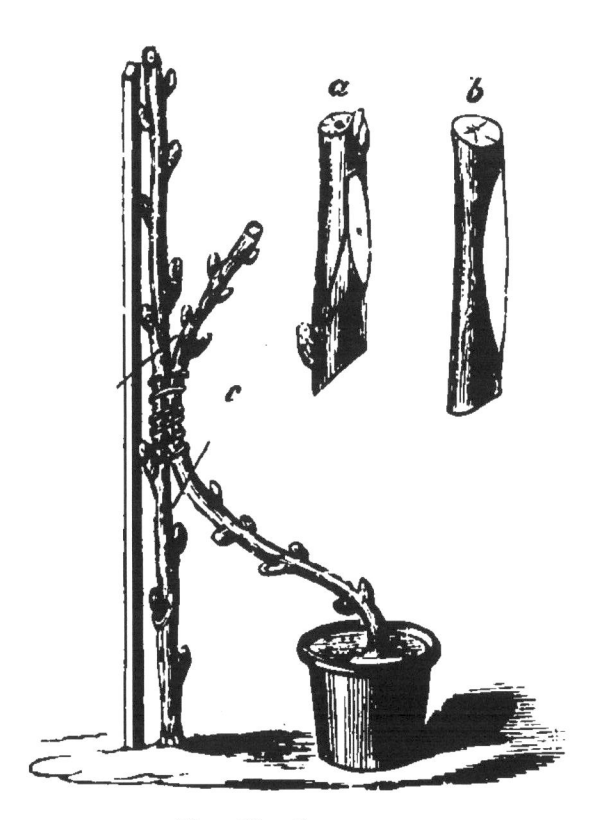

FIG. 21. INARCHING.

shoots is restricted to one on the pot plant. Choose the height of the stock and scion where the union is to take place; then place the pot in such a position that the scion will reach the desired height, and make the pot secure, so that the scion cannot afterwards slip from its position when connected to the vine. With a sharp knife remove from both parts intended for joining together a portion of the bark, as represented by *a* and *b* in the engraving (Fig. 21), some from the young wood and a similar piece from the underneath side of the existing vine, so that the two connections join evenly together, it being essential for the bark to meet at one side and at the bottom at least, but preferably all round. When the junction is complete, the parts must be carefully bound round with soft bast to connect the two securely, so that the union may be perfect. It is well to apply a thin layer of grafting-wax, so that neither air nor water can get to the connection, and care should be taken that the binding is not done so tightly as to bruise the bark, but yet firm enough to make all secure. The bark should be dry that the wax may adhere well; and the work should be done neatly and quickly, that the surfaces may not become dry, or the labour will be in vain.

In a very short time it will be seen by the extended growth of the scion that a union has taken place. The roots in the pot must be regularly supplied with water in the same manner as though it were still dependent upon its own roots for sustenance; in fact, it is so until it has become thoroughly established upon the vine. When it is thought by the amount of growth made that a thorough union has been secured, the bast which bound the two together must be removed, but in a careful manner, that the scion be not pulled off the stock again. If the bast is left on too long, the bark will not grow evenly on either the stock or the scion.

When pruning the vines in winter is a good time to sever the stock from the scion, as shown by the lines at c (Fig. 21); and the growth during the first year should be restricted to the one shoot, removing all lateral growths, and allowing the leader to extend its full length.

CHAPTER XXI.

RENOVATING OLD BORDERS.

MANY vines which are in an apparently exhausted condition are simply suffering from causes which can be remedied, such as growing in borders which are too deep, or made of the wrong kind of soil, or badly drained, or with some other defect which tends to interfere with their healthy growth. But borders which labour under any or all of these disadvantages can be renovated in either of two ways: one consisting in the entire removal of the soil and rectification of the drainage, the other plan being to remove the surface soil, so that the roots may be brought to the top of the border, whence they may have been driven by a variety of causes, such as lack of moisture, or the presence of much manure in the soil, which give a downward tendency to the roots.

If a vine border happens to be made too deep, say from 3ft. to 4ft. of soil and drainage below that, there will be no cause for wonder if the vines fail to perfect their crop of grapes. When this is the case, it is the best plan to re-make the border, filling up the surplus space with drainage—stones, broken bricks, or whatever is handiest in that way—allowing only the depth of soil advised in the chapter on Borders, page 11. But should there be a combination of inside and outside borders, only one should be taken in hand in a season, and it matters little whether it be the inside or the outside one which is done first. Where there is one border only for the one set of vines, it will not be possible to secure a crop of fruit in the season following that in which the border is re-made; but where a combination of inside and outside borders are employed, the entire crop of grapes need not be lost, as the border unmolested, if it is pretty well supplied with healthy roots, will enable the vines to carry a moderate crop of fruit.

I should advise any cultivator who cannot succeed with his vines, owing to the defective state of the border, to set about the renewal of this immediately the season for it arrives, even if a season's crop of fruit has to be sacrificed; and the improvement which will manifest itself in the vines afterwards, if the work be carried out properly, will well repay the inconvenience and loss of crop for one year. The best way to set about the work is thus: If the vinery is provided with inside and outside borders, directly the grapes are cut — say early in October — is the best time to carry out the work; and should the vines be late-fruiting kinds, it would be even better to cut and bottle the grapes at the time named rather than wait longer, as the grapes, no matter what kind, would be ripe by this time, and would consequently keep as well cut and bottled as if left on the vines. The advantage of renewing the borders thus early in the season is that the roots will have an opportunity of making a fresh start before the winter actually sets in. If, however, the house is provided with one border only—it matters little whether it be inside or outside the vinery—it would not be wise, perhaps, to lift the vines entirely until the leaves fall off naturally.

Commence to remove the soil at the extreme end of the border, employing a steel digging-fork, so that the roots will not be broken off or otherwise damaged. As the work proceeds and the roots are bared, cover them with wet mats, occasionally syringing them to keep them moist, as if allowed to become dry injury would be caused to the vines. If the leaves of the vines show signs of flagging owing to the disturbance of the roots in one of the borders and a strong sun, which at that time of the year is often powerful, shade the outside of the roof with mats or anything else which will have the desired effect. Well syringe the vines in the evening, to keep the foliage as fresh as possible. Any bare fibreless roots should be cut at not more than 3ft. from the stem of the vine, as this will induce fibrous roots to form, bare ones being almost useless as feeders to the vine.

The roots should be kept as near to the surface as possible; owing to their bent shape, however, and the manner in which they previously grew, it will sometimes happen that they cannot very well be laid near the surface of the border. In this case spread them evenly among the soil, laying them out as straight as possible, and put on a layer of soil, making it firm as the work proceeds; and continue in this way until all are laid in the desired position. Those nearest the top need not be more than 2in. under the surface of the border. The soil should be moist when used, and water will not then be required for at least ten days; but if it is on the dry side, give sufficient water to moisten all the roots two or three days after the border is re-made. No more water should be needed until the following March, which is quite soon enough to start the vines into growth for the next season, as forcing would be too much of a strain upon them after having their roots so much interfered with. Directly the leaves regain their freshness, should they have shown signs of flagging, remove the shade from the glass, but occasionally moisten them in the afternoon of each day.

It may not be convenient, perhaps, to do more than raise the roots near the surface of the border. In that case, the method of proceeding is the same—*i.e.*, carefully removing the top soil, preserving all the roots possible and maintaining them in a moist state, and also syringing the vines occasionally. By thus only partially renewing the border, the next season's crop of fruit will not be nearly so much interfered with; but it is not wise to crop too heavily, even then. The vines will recover sooner from the slight check, which they are sure to receive, when carrying a light crop of fruit, than they will if loaded with too many bunches; and when there is a heavy strain put upon the vines by the weight of fruit retained, their future prospects cannot be so good.

No variety of grapes shows its appreciation of this root-raising more than does the Muscat of Alexandria, rightly named the "Prince of Grapes," the subsequent improvement in growth being always remarkable.

The advantages of raising the roots near to the surface are manifold; increased warmth being a great point in its favour, while the ease with which they can be fed is worth some consideration, as the roots near the surface are of the greatest value to the vine as feeders.

CHAPTER XXII.

PECULIARITIES OF SOME VARIETIES.

THERE are some sorts of grapes which need treatment different to most others to bring them to perfection, and many of these are well worthy of extra trouble to gain the desired effect. Take, for instance, that grand variety Madresfield Court, which under correct cultivation produces both massive and shapely bunches, as well as being of exquisite flavour. Grown in the manner that would produce fair Black Hamburgh and very good Foster's Seedling or Alicante, for instance, Madresfield Court would fail to perfect a single bunch, perhaps owing to the special treatment that it requires at various stages of its growth. Then, again, such handsome-looking kinds as Duke of Buccleuch and Gros Guillaume, acknowledged shy-bearing kinds, both need a deviation from the orthodox style before they can be had in perfection as to quality and quantity.

Taking first Madresfield Court, more persons would cultivate this variety than do so at the present time if its wants were better understood, although this sort has one serious fault—that of its berries splitting across the point. Where this is in existense in a bad way the whole crop of fruit is ruined, for that year at any rate. Madresfield Court is a grape of easy culture to those who understand its peculiarities and know how to deal with it under all phases of its culture; and its quality is so high when at its best that I consider it advisable to point out not only its great peculiarity, but also how to deal with it, so that amateur cultivators may be enabled to grow this fine sort as well as their professional brethren, who generally have many more facilities at command.

As before stated, the splitting of the berries across the point just at the time when colouring commences is the great drawback to the cultivation of Madresfield Court. Many are the reasons assigned for the defective finishing of the berries, such as keeping the atmosphere of the house too moist and the roots too wet; others, again, say the plant ought to have a house to itself, so that the roots could be kept in whatever state thought best, which cannot be done when it is growing in a mixed house. My experience, however, does not lead me to the conclusion that it is necessary for it to be grown by itself to reap a measure of success; for I find it very accommodating as to position, growing well with other kinds and receiving the same atmospheric treatment as they do. I grow it in a house which ripens Black Hamburgh at the end of June, and in another house mainly planted with late sorts, such as Lady Downes, Alicante, and the like—these ripening towards the end of September, while the Madresfield Court is ready to cut about a month earlier; and for the last ten years I have had no reason to complain about its cracking propensities. I do not mean to say I have never had a single berry which has cracked during that time, but all so damaged could be counted on the fingers of two hands; and as the treatment has always been the same, I have reason for sticking to the method which gives such results. In my opinion, it is the thinness of skin of the berries, when compared with the amount of sap the variety is charged with, that is the chief cause of their splitting; and when the shoots are restricted in the manner adopted with most other sorts, the berries are not capable of assimilating the excess of sap, as other sorts do, because of the thinness of their skins. No variety that I know has such a thin skin as Madresfield Court.

Where the vines are healthy, the berries swell at a rapid rate when they commence after stoning, and no grape more so;

the foliage and the growth of laterals, too, being made in the same proportion. Then is the time to apply the remedy, which is the extension of laterals at the time the fruit is taking its second swelling, to prepare the berries to withstand the pressure put upon them at a later stage, when they commence to colour. The lateral growth should be allowed to extend at will, particularly from the leaders; and in the case of young vines this can easily be done, as more roof space is available and the extra growth does not crowd the main foliage upon the side branches, which would prevent each main leaf performing its necessary function. By this means the superfluity of sap, so to speak, finds space without interfering with the proper swelling of the berries. Thus, by allowing a free extension of lateral growth at the time named, the evil of splitting is remedied.

The amateur must not think, however, that the moment the berries commence to swell after the stoning process is complete *all* lateral growth upon the vines, whether they be young or old, must be allowed to extend, perhaps in some cases to the detriment of the main foliage; for though the departure from the orthodox plan of stopping the shoots must be considerable, under no circumstances must the vines be allowed to grow wild, so to speak. The lateral growths must not so overcrowd the main leaves on the side branches that they will not be able to do what is required of them in supporting the vines, because from these main leaves much of the support which the vines require is obtained; but wherever there is space the laterals must be allowed to extend, even at the expense of crowding each other a little, until the crucial time has past and the berries have coloured thoroughly and ceased to swell. Cracking never takes place after that stage. Therefore it will be seen that the amateur cultivator must, after all, use a little discretion in the management of his vines of this sort.

Of course it would be of no use to allow the laterals to extend if other details of culture were not considered also, such as supplying the roots *properly* with water, to enable the berries to swell to their proper size; for a too wet border, with the roots inactive and an atmosphere constantly laden with moisture, will cause the same defect. The atmosphere of the house should be kept in a buoyant state, by airing freely in suitable weather, especially early in the morning, to prevent the temperature rising unduly while the atmosphere of the house is charged with moisture. This should be dissipated gradually by the admission of air, judiciously increasing the supply as the temperature of the house demands it. In the case of wet or dull weather, the hot-water pipes should be made warm, as this keeps the air in free circulation, driving out any moisture which might otherwise condense on the berries.

At the time the berries commence to colour the borders should be watered sufficiently to carry the vines through the colouring process, although there is no need to be afraid of watering the inside borders while colouring is progressing if there is a sufficiency of lateral growth extension, and provided also that the water is not applied to the borders at a time when the outside elements do not admit of air being given to the house at the time of watering. After sufficient water has been given to the borders to carry the crops through the colouring stage, it is a good plan to mulch the surface of the inside one with clean straw, which prevents moisture rising from it, as this may condense and settle on the berries, causing some on the inside of the bunch to decay when ripe. This may occur, too, through neglecting to supply a sufficiency of air to the house.

Some suggest as a preventive of splitting the keeping of the borders, both inside and outside (where a combination are employed), in a somewhat dry state at the time the berries begin to colour. I do not recommend this plan, as a too dry border at this period prevents the berries swelling to their proper size, neither do they colour nearly so well; while vines so treated are liable to be attacked by red-spider, this variety being particularly liable to the attacks of that insect. In fact, it is impossible to have Madresfield Court in proper condition under such circumstances. Should red-spider have gained a footing on the leaves—and it is sure to be the leaves nearest to the main stem which are attacked first—additional lateral growth should be allowed to extend, to provide shade in the absence of the main leaves damaged by the pest.

Other persons assert that the cutting of the branches half-way through below the bunches, so as to cause the sap to flow less hurriedly to them, will prevent the splitting of the berries. I have tried this on some branches, but found the bunches on them split, while others on the same vine which were not cut at all did not split in the least; therefore I attach no importance to this plan.

I have seen bad cases of the berries splitting where the vine had been inarched on another sort, while in the same garden, on a vine growing on its own roots, the berries did not split at all; but whether this case of splitting was due to faulty treatment atmospherically, I am unable to say. In any case, having found that own-root vines of Madresfield Court perfect full crops of good fruit without splitting, I do not see the necessity of inarching on to another stock.

In addition to allowing an extension of lateral growth, directly the berries commence to colour, if there are signs of much rain, the outside border (ours being a combination) is covered with lights from the frames, boards or other temporary coverings, to guard against thunder- or other heavy showers, which might, by causing an over-wet state of the roots, induce the berries to split.

Gros Guillaume, sometimes called Barbarossa, is another variety which fails to succeed under the orthodox method adopted with other kinds, its weakness lying in its inability to produce yearly a sufficient number of bunches to secure a full crop of fruit; for although six of the large bunches which this sort sometimes produces would be considered a full crop for any vine, no matter how strong it might be—because they often weigh from 6lb. to 10lb. each, and in some instances more—plenty of vines after the first six years will not produce above half of that number when pruned on the close-spur system. Where exhibition or sensational bunches are required, Barbarossa is a good sort to cultivate, for in spite of their size they are as a rule quite symmetrical in form, and when not cropped too heavily the berries both attain a large size and colour well.

To succeed yearly with this sort, the pruning should be carried out on a slightly different plan to that which is practised on vines which are free-fruiting—as for instance Alicante. Thus, instead of pruning the current year's growth to within one or two eyes, every third branch on each side should be cut to within four or five buds of the stem, selecting one which is stout and plump, and the intermediate spurs should be pruned to within one eye of the main rod; these will produce the branches for next year's crop of fruit, and will be dealt with in their turn like those previously described. By adopting this plan of pruning, a third year's crop of fruit is provided. After the shoots have borne fruit, they should be cut back close to the main stem, or nearly so, and growths will in time spring from this place, to provide shoots for a future crop of fruit.

Duke of Buccleuch is another variety which has a similar peculiarity to Gros Guillaume in the matter of bunch producing, and similar treatment should be accorded to it in pruning, the only exception being that more long spurs must be left, as the bunches do not nearly approach those of Gros Guillaume in size. Every second shoot should be depended upon to produce bunches. The value of this grape lies in its being a good white variety which forces well, this class of grape not being over plentiful; in addition to this, the berries attain an enormous size, and on this account, too, it is much appreciated. Certainly, when seen in the best condition, it is a grape to admire.

CHAPTER XXIII.

LIQUID STIMULANTS DURING WINTER.

TO many amateurs this heading will appear a strange one, I have no doubt, and they will think, How can vines require stimulants during the winter months? I will endeavour to point out how vines are benefited by stimulative food being given during the winter in a liquid form. It is not with young vines that I propose to deal, nor with those the roots of which are growing in an outside border, but with vines that have grown old and are in need of all the stimulative food that can be given to them, especially when the roots are confined to an inside border which has not been properly provided with a retaining wall. In that case, the roots will have rambled away underneath the floor of the vinery and about the brickwork of the centre staging with which old vineries, in which numbers of other plants have to be cultivated, are often fitted. In such a case as this, liquid stimulants are an advantage to the vines.

Any time during the winter, after the leaves have fallen, all available places should be examined, and the soil underneath the paths and elsewhere—not actually in the border—be thoroughly soaked with liquid manure from the farmyard tank, if such be available. A few bricks here and there in the path might be removed where they are laid on sand or soil only, as very often such places are found to be full of healthy roots, which cannot possibly derive any nourishment from the soil itself. By thoroughly soaking the soil under the path and elsewhere with liquid manure, the roots will be much improved, and the following season's growth will be considerably the better for this winter application.

CHAPTER XXIV.

MULTIPLICATION OF BRANCHES.

IN the case of a vine turning out unsatisfactorily, instead of going to the trouble and expense of planting a new one in the place of it, or taking the trouble of inarching another and more suitable one on to the defaulter, there is a way by which both of these plans may be avoided, viz.: the multiplication of the branches of the vine nearest to the discarded one, providing of course the next vine is an approved sort. An extra rod must be secured from the existing cane of that variety which it is desired to increase. Instead of stopping the shoot two leaves or so beyond the bunch, as is usually done, allow the growth which springs from the bottom spur of the neighbouring vine to grow away uninterruptedly until it reaches three-parts of the way up the rafter to the top of the vinery, treating it in a similar way to a young vine in the matter of manipulation of lateral and sub-lateral growths. The training of the shoot must start early in the season, or the right form will not be easy to obtain afterwards. The shoot should be trained first in a horizontal manner, until the position it is eventually to occupy is reached, when it should be gradually bent in an upward position as near at a right angle as possible. Of course it will not be policy to attempt to train it into the exact form all at once, or the sappy growth might snap right off at a joint, thus ruining the year's growth or nearly so, and certainly the shape which it was intended to occupy would be interfered with. By gentle persuasion and carefully securing the shoot to the wires, an easy bend may be obtained the first season. Treat it afterwards in exactly the same manner as recommended in Chapter XII. for the First Year's Growth. Such varieties as Black Hamburgh, Madresfield Court, Lady Downes, Gros Colman, Muscat of Alexandria, and Mrs. Pince, succeed admirably with several rods to each vine.

CHAPTER XXV.

AIR ROOTS.

I HAVE heard many amateurs ask why air roots, as they are termed, are produced upon vines which from their general appearance are in perfect health. The question is not so easily answered as some might imagine, because they are to be found upon vines which succeed admirably in every respect; and this fact upsets the argument of some cultivators, that vines which produce these adventitious roots are not in a condition of health to perfect a crop of grapes. There is no doubt, however, but that vines which succeed without these roots are to be preferred to others which annually produce them from 6in. to 1ft. in length.

My opinion is that they are the result of a scarcity of fibrous roots to the vines in the border, this condition being brought about by the coldness of the soil, which is in itself a consequence of its retentive nature. Vines growing in such a soil very often lose many of their quill-like roots during the winter, these having only recently been made during the latter part of the summer. When the vines are growing in a warm moist temperature, nature asserts itself by providing such vines with other roots in compensation for those lost. The vines, really, have not sufficient time to make new roots the following season before others are driven, so to speak, out of the canes in quest of moisture.

Where many of these air roots have been present upon

vines which I have inspected, I have also noted some shanked berries, which are more often caused by defective root action than anything else; therefore, the two circumstances coincide exactly.

I do not know whether it is wise to cut off air roots when they appear, but I think not, as I am inclined to the opinion that they are of service to the vines, as they surely absorb much moisture from the air, which cannot fail to do good rather than harm. As the moisture in the vinery is reduced upon the approach of autumn, and the vines are ripening, the roots die off; then they should be cut away for the sake of appearance.

Black Hamburgh is perhaps more prone to the production of adventitious roots than any other variety, and is also perhaps more given to shanking in the berries than any other sort cultivated, excepting perhaps Muscat of Hamburgh, which is notorious for this fault.

The only cure there is, in my opinion, lays in the re-making of the border and encouraging the vines to make roots freely near its surface; but I do not think that vines, which succeed otherwise, should be disturbed merely because of th appearance of air roots.

INDEX.

Air roots, 121
Alicante variety, 25
Alnwick Seedling variety, 27
August, varieties to ripen in, 30

Barbarossa variety, 26, 115
Berries, rust on, 82
    scalding of, 83
Black Hamburgh variety, 23
    Morocco variety, 27
    varieties, 23
Bleeding, 95
Borders and soil, 11
    renovating old, 107
Bottling grapes, 88
Branches, multiplication of, 119
Buckland Sweetwater variety, 28
Bunches, supporting shoulders of, 74
    thinning, 67

Cannon Hall Muscat variety, 29
Compost, 14
Conservatory treatment, 47
    varieties, 30
Cuttings, propagation by, 16

Diseases and pests, 67
Double-bud method of pruning, 98
Draining borders, 13
Duchess of Buccleuch variety, 29
Duke of Buccleuch variety, 29

Early varieties, 30
    vinery treatment, 36
Eyes, propagation by, 16

First year's growth of young vines, 56
Forms of vineries, 4
Foster's Seedling variety, 28

Glass houses, 4
Golden Queen variety, 29
Greenhouse and vinery combined, 9
    treatment, 47
    varieties, 30
Gros Colman variety, 25
Gros Guillaume variety, 26
Gros Maroc variety, 27

Hamburgh, Black, variety, 23
    Mill Hill, variety, 28
    Muscat, variety, 26
Heating, 8
Hot-water pipes, distribution of, 8
Houses, forms of, 4

Inarching, 104
Introduction, 1

June, varieties to ripen in, 30

Lady Downes variety, 24
Late-keeping varieties, 31
Late vinery, treatment, 43
Lean-to vinery, 4
Leaves, warts on underside of, 83
Liquid stimulants during winter, 117
List of varieties, 22

Madresfield Court variety, 24
Manure, 54, 117

INDEX.

Mildew, 81
Mill Hill Hamburgh variety, 28
Morocco, Black, variety, 27
Mrs. Pince variety, 26
Mulching, 55
Multiplication of branches, 119
Muscat vinery treatment, 40
  Hamburgh variety, 26
  of Alexandria variety, 28

Oidium Tuckeri, 81
Outdoor culture, 2
  varieties, 30

Pests and diseases, 77
Pipes, distribution of, 8
Planting, 32
Pots for propagation, 17
Pot vines, 36
Propagation, 16, 104
Pruning, 93

Red spider, 77
Renovating old borders, 107
Roots, air, 121
  disposition of, 34
Rust on the berries, 82

Scalding of the berries, 83
Shanking, 84
Shoots, manipulation of, 63

Soil and borders, 9
Span-roof vinery, 7
Spider, 77
Stopping shoots, 64
Summer treatment, 49
Supporting shoulders of bunches, 74
Syringing, 53

Tetranychus telarius, 77
Thinning bunches, 67
Three-quarter-span vinery, 5
Thrips, 80
Trebbiano variety, 30
Trentham Black variety, 27

Varieties, list of, 23
  peculiarities of some, 111
Ventilation, 52
Vineries, forms of, 4

Warts on under-side of leaves, 83
Washing houses and vines, 100
Watering, 49
White Frontignan variety, 29
  Tokay variety, 30
  varieties, 28
Winter, liquid stimulants during, 117
  treatment, 99
Wires for fixing vines to rafters,

Manufactured by Amazon.ca
Bolton, ON